DAILY PRAYER *for* TIMES OF GRIEF

LISA B. HAMILTON

DAILY PRAYER *for* TIMES OF GRIEF

LISA B. HAMILTON

PARACLETE PRESS
BREWSTER, MASSACHUSETTS

Daily Prayer for Times of Grief

2012 First and Second Printing

©2001 by The Rev. Lisa Belcher Hamilton
ISBN: 978-1-55725-271-5

Scripture quotations designated (NJB) are taken from The New Jerusalem
Bible, ©1985 by Darton, Longman & Todd, Ltd. and Doubleday, a
division of Random House, Inc. Reprinted by permission.

Scripture quotations designated (KJV) are taken from the King James
Version of the Bible.

Scripture quotations designated (NRSV) are taken from the New Revised
Standard Version of the Bible, ©1989, by the Division of Christian
Education of the National Council of the Churches of Christ in the USA.
All rights reserved. Used by permission.

Scripture quotations designated (NIV) are taken from the Holy Bible,
New International Version. NIV. ©1973, 1978, 1984 by International
Bible Society. Used by permission of Zondervan Publishing House. All
rights reserved.

The Library of Congress has cataloged the original edition of *For Those We
Love But See No Longer* as follows:

Hamilton, Lisa Belcher, 1959–
  For those we love but see no longer : Daily Offices for times of grief /
  Lisa Belcher Hamilton.
        p. cm.
Includes bibliographical references.
    ISBN 1-55725-271-8 (pbk.)
  1. Bereavement—Prayer-books and devotions—English.   2.
Consolation—Prayer-books and devotions—English. I. Title.
    BV4905.2 .H355 2001
    242′.4—dc21
00–012923

10 9 8 7 6 5 4 3 2

Published by Paraclete Press
Brewster, Massachusetts
www.paracletepress.com

Printed in the United States of America.

For Scott Lane Hamilton
(1959–1991)
A man of God who pursued righteousness,
godliness, faith, love, endurance, gentleness.

Fight the good fight of the faith;
take hold of the eternal life, to which you
were called and for which you
made the good confession.
I TIMOTHY 6:12 (NRSV)

TABLE OF CONTENTS

INTRODUCTION

Our son was 26 months old the perfect June night he discovered lightning bugs. I can't count the times I've tried to bring back the conversation his Dada and I were having when he interrupted us to pry open his chubby fingers and see the bug glow green, then stop, then glow green again. "Look Dada, see bug light!" Teddy squealed, and with every ounce of his being, Scott helped him into his lap. They took turns holding the last gift Teddy gave his father.

When Scott had cancer, Teddy was forever giving him things—even his precious "yanyee," his much-snuggled blue blanket. When there was nothing on hand, Teddy "made" things. The morning of a chemotherapy treatment, we walked our dog to the park, where Teddy interrupted his climbing long enough to make and feed Scott pretend oatmeal. But nothing anyone could give him cured the cancer. It took death.

Death came the night Teddy discovered lightning bugs. Scott passed out as he tried to climb the stairs in our "starter house," and I dragged him to the bed crying, "I won't let you fall, I won't let you fall, I won't let you fall." I jabbered and prayed aloud until he opened his eyes and croaked out, "I love you." He even regained enough strength to say Compline with me. We kissed goodnight, and in the morning, we were still holding hands, but his was dead.

Everything was different that morning, including the way God was speaking to me in Psalm 91—the Psalm we always chose at Compline. Psalm 91 was one of the ways God broke through the cancer to teach us to pray together. Psalm 91, with its images of safety under God's wings, of refuge in angels' hands, promised us that there was no terror even in plague. It was the last psalm of Scott's life—and yet God did not "rescue him and bring him to honor." The last verse—"With long life will I satisfy him, and show him to salvation"—had once helped bring us the relief of sleep. Only after a few years of accusing God of betrayal did I come to realize that, for Scott, the psalm's promises are for eternity.

My being changed by the unchanging words of Psalm 91 is a discovery as ancient as the psalms themselves. Indeed, so is being changed by praying at fixed times of day. The psalms are often called "Jesus' prayers" because they were (and are) such an integral part of Jewish worship. Jews were expected to pray at fixed hours, and it's interesting to note how many important New Testament events occur at these times of prayer, as when Peter and John healed the lame man (Acts 3:1–10) who was lying at the "Beautiful Gate" of the Temple; the apostles were entering for prayer at three in the afternoon.

Apparently it took some centuries for Christians to settle on a schedule of fixed prayer, with early writers advocating prayer three or five or seven times a day. All schedules, however, included prayer at sunrise and sunset. Today's Offices (the term comes from the Latin *opus Dei*, meaning "work of God") place us in communion with the earliest believers, as several elements (including the psalms and the Lord's Prayer) were used from the beginnings of our faith, although scriptural readings were not used in daily prayer, but saved for the Sunday Eucharist and other select occasions. By the mid-sixth century, the Daily Offices included Scripture, and due in large part to St. Benedict, were fixed in a shape that is familiar to Christians today. The seven Benedictine Hours are collapsed in *The Book of Common Prayer* into Morning Prayer, Noontime Prayer, Vespers or Evening Prayer, and Compline, so the ancient structure and content connect not only with the living who pray them, but with the dead who have prayed them as well.

Perhaps grief has brought you to regulated prayer because you may find that structure helps you cope with the day. I did not return to work for some time after Scott's death, and I remember my relief at devising a schedule that ensured Teddy and I would be out of the house for a time every day. On Tuesdays, a plaster handprint recalls, we attended a "Mommy and Me" art class. I made certain that every day, we saw other people, even if they were strangers in the grocery store, and this was important. But the Daily Offices offer a holy connection to an unbroken chain of Christians—and provide us with deeper nourishment than we can devise alone.

When someone we love dies, it is often very painful to move to a new place. I remember the day of the Pittsburgh tag sale a year after Scott died because Teddy and I were moving to New Haven, Connecticut, where I would enter Yale Divinity School. As I saw people carrying away things I'd sold them, I felt as if I were watching our life disappear down the driveway. I've never found it comfortable to move in any way—geographically, professionally, emotionally—and now, without Scott, I feel I am somehow being disloyal in moving. Saying familiar prayers in a familiar form is a security I can take from job to job, from home to home, from feeling to feeling, and the knowledge that Scott and I are linked in prayer has often brought me the feeling that he is proud of the moving I do.

Prayer is the most lasting way I know to cope with loneliness. In part, grief is lonely because there are so few people able to listen without wanting to "make it all better." One particularly bad day the summer Scott died, the phone rang, and when I said "Hello," I was greeted with, "You sound so much better. It's great that you're happy again." I spent the rest of the forgotten conversation staring at the front porch and wondering how I could sound better, and even happy, when the newspapers were piling up because I didn't have any interest in reading them.

Therapists would call my caller's comments "projection"—projecting onto me an image of what he wanted me to be. Projection is impossible in prayer, because prayer can offer a glimpse of ourselves and our lives through the eyes of God. In my experience, this level of prayer occurs most frequently when I am in the habit of praying so regularly that as the Rev. Suzanne Guthrie describes it, "Your soul becomes alert in anticipation, just as your stomach does if you eat at noon every day."[1] Committing yourself to regulated prayer in grief offers you a nourishing structure in difficult days and clears the way for a more honest knowledge of God, yourself, and your relationships with God and your loved one.

Fixed-time prayer offers us a larger purpose than learning to live with our own pain. As Phyllis Tickle describes it, "Like relay runners passing a lighted torch, those who do the work of fixed-hour prayer do create thereby a continuous cascade of praise before the throne of God."[2] The eight cancer months Scott and I shared, similar to our pregnancy months, were filled with purpose. The purpose was to poison the cancer, reverse the metastases, and pray a cure, ignoring the odds as stubbornly as we curled in hospital beds together, nursing Teddy as the chemotherapy dripped medical hope through Scott's body.

However difficult it was to realize that the purpose of prayer is to align oneself with God's will rather than hammer away on the merits of one's own desires, praying returned purpose to me. Imperceptibly, I began to pray for those beyond Scott, Teddy, and me. Prayer expands me still, as if I am a bowl being shaped by a potter. I am large enough to pray for a teenage friend in trouble, relatives I do not understand, people in car accidents—even when the accident is making me late for work. Prayer seems to welcome the stranger, so that reports from the morning news often find their way into noontime prayer.

I've worked on *Daily Prayer for Times of Grief* envisioning people silently praying on subways, because it was on New York's Lexington line that I first prayed intentionally, with the help of *Morning and Evening Prayer with Selected Psalms and Readings for the Church Year*.[3] I'm hopeful that *Daily Prayer for Times of Grief* can also be used for praying aloud, in groups of people as well as alone. The good people at Paraclete have designed this book to be small enough to carry with you in purse or pocket, and with the help of the Good Paraclete, I hope it will provide you with a way to live days of grief. Praying at rising, noon, evening, and retiring with the Daily Office links us to other Christians who engage in this common and ancient spiritual practice, and so we are less alone than we may feel. I've chosen readings and prayers for their purpose, variety, and faithfulness, and set them in the security and community of the Daily Offices as found in *The Book of Common Prayer*. Although this book is in no way intended to replace *The Book of Common Prayer*, it is nevertheless comforting to recall that Thomas Cranmer, chief architect of *The Book of Common Prayer*, began his work after losing his wife and their baby in childbirth.

I've selected Morning Prayer readings to help the griever face another day without those who are dead. Noonday readings are a cry of missing the dead, "whom we love but see no longer," as *The Book of Common Prayer* puts it so poignantly in a prayer suggested for burial.[4] Evening Prayer readings offer hope for the dead. At Compline, readings commend both oneself and the dead to God. Fridays are focused on God's grief at the crucifixion of Christ.

When used individually, the Office may be said silently or aloud. When used by a group, longer sections are divided so that each person or group takes turns. Lines to be read by the leader are followed by an asterisk (*). Group responses are indented and follow the asterisk.

All texts, including the Psalms, are excerpted from *The Book of Common Prayer* unless otherwise noted. Many of these texts have been adapted for this book. Such texts are indicated by the symbol †.

There is space for journaling at the end of each day, in the hope that your journaling can teach you about your grief—and therefore about yourself. You may want to write letters, to God, to your loved one, or even to yourself. Or perhaps writing prayers will feel more natural to you. At least sometimes, you may find yourself drawing. Whatever form or forms you use, dating your entries or even making an index will make your journaling more helpful to you over time.

Given that grief does not leave within seven days, you may wonder why *Daily Prayer for Times of Grief* provides only one week of Offices. First of all, I want this book to be portable: small enough to pray within a subway car. Second, I hope this will be a book you use as needed. There may be days or weeks at a time when your prayer feels more honest when you rely on the tried and true *Book of Common Prayer*, or when you utilize another form of prayer. To this end, I've recommended several books to which you may "graduate" or which you may wish to incorporate as supplementary even while using *Daily Prayer for Times of Grief*.

If you're familiar with the Daily Offices, you'll notice immediately that the Confession is missing from those in *Daily Prayer for Times of Grief*. If you feel that saying the Confession is helpful to you, by all means include it—the Rite II Confession from *The Book of Common Prayer* can be found at the end of this book.

My reason for excluding the Confession in *Daily Prayer for Times of Grief* is that Scott's death erupted a fireworks of guilt for me, and I suspect it may be common for a long period of time to need to pass before saying the Confession is helpful. Nevertheless, the Confession I so seldom said for so long was useful to me in bringing me closer to God through anger. Even now the Confession sometimes raises for me the question of whether God causes pain purposelessly. If God is omnipotent, isn't God culpable for cancer and all the pain it unleashes?

Many times, I've said the Confession with my mouth while raging in my heart: "Who should be confessing to whom, God?" I've learned that times when my anger might be judged blasphemous seem to be used particularly well by God to deepen our relationship. As a wise friend of mine notes, "God doesn't cast us off because of our anger." Thank God.

When Scott was very ill, I faced a priest across our backyard picnic table and asked, "Is this happening because God *can't* stop it or because God *won't* stop it?" Two divinity school degrees later, I'm still searching for the reason(s) suffering and God cohabit our lives. The intersection seems to be nowhere other than the cross. When you find yourself at the cross, I pray that *Daily Prayer for Times of Grief* will help you to remember that as lonely as Golgotha is, it is not a place where we are alone. Jesus' arms were nailed in a posture of embrace on the cross, and they are spread for us in fixed welcome. May prayer help you embrace his welcome.

MONDAY

MONDAY MORNING PRAYER

※

THE INVITATION TO WORSHIP

Out of the deep have I called unto thee, O Lord: *
Lord, hear my voice.

The Lord is full of compassion and mercy: *
Come, let us adore him.

Glory to the Father, and to the Son, and to the
Holy Spirit: * as it was in the beginning, is now,
and will be for ever. Amen.

PSALM 86:1–13

Bow down your ear, O LORD, and answer me, * for I
am poor and in misery.

Keep watch over my life, for I am faithful; * save
your servant who puts his trust in you.

Be merciful to me, O LORD, for you are my God; * I
call upon you all the day long.

Gladden the soul of your servant, * for to you, O
LORD, I lift up my soul.

For you, O LORD, are good and forgiving, * and
great is your love toward all who call upon you.

Give ear, O LORD, to my prayer, * and attend to
the voice of my supplications.

In the time of my trouble I will call upon you, * for
you will answer me.

Among the gods there is none like you, O LORD, *
    nor anything like your works.
All nations you have made will come and worship
    you, O LORD, * and glorify your Name.
For you are great; you do wondrous things; * and
    you alone are God.
Teach me your way, O LORD, and I will walk in
    your truth; * knit my heart to you that I may
    fear your Name.
I will thank you, O LORD my God, with all my
    heart, * and glorify your Name for evermore.
For great is your love toward me; * you have
    delivered me from the nethermost Pit.
Glory to the Father, and to the Son, and to the
    Holy Spirit: * as it was in the beginning, is now,
    and will be for ever. Amen.

THE WORD

Then fixing his eyes on his disciples he said:
    How blessed are you who are poor:
    the kingdom of God is yours.
    Blessed are you who are hungry now:
    you shall have your fill.
    Blessed are you who are weeping now:
    you shall laugh.

LUKE 6:20–21 (NJB)

Thanks be to God.

CANTICLE
THE FIRST SONG OF ISAIAH, ISAIAH 12:2–5

Surely, it is God who saves me; * I will trust in him
and not be afraid.

For the Lord is my stronghold and my sure
defense, * and he will be my Savior.

Therefore you shall draw water with rejoicing *
from the springs of salvation.

And on that day you shall say, * Give thanks to
the Lord and call upon his Name;

Make his deeds known among the peoples; * see
that they remember that his Name is exalted.

Sing the praises of the Lord, for he has done great
things, * and this is known in all the world.†

Glory to the Father, and to the Son, and to the
Holy Spirit: * as it was in the beginning, is now,
and will be for ever. Amen.

THE APOSTLES' CREED

I believe in God, the Father almighty, creator of
heaven and earth.

I believe in Jesus Christ, his only Son, our Lord.
He was conceived by the power of the
Holy Spirit and born of the Virgin Mary.
He suffered under Pontius Pilate, was
crucified, died, and was buried.
He descended to the dead.

On the third day he rose again.
He ascended into heaven, and is seated at
the right hand of the Father.
He will come again to judge the living and
the dead.
I believe in the Holy Spirit, the holy catholic
Church, the communion of saints, the
forgiveness of sins, the resurrection of the
body, and the life everlasting. Amen.

THE PRAYERS

Our Father in heaven,
hallowed be your Name,
your kingdom come,
your will be done,
on earth as in heaven.
Give us today our daily bread.
Forgive us our sins
as we forgive those
who sin against us.
Save us from the time of trial,
and deliver us from evil.
For the kingdom, the power,
and the glory are yours,
now and for ever. Amen.

THE PETITIONS

Show us your mercy, O Lord; *
    And grant us your salvation.
Clothe your ministers with righteousness; *
    Let your people sing with joy.
Give peace, O Lord, in all the world; *
    For only in you can we live in safety.
Lord, keep this nation under your care; *
    And guide us in the way of justice and truth.
Let your way be known upon earth; *
    Your saving health among all nations.
Let not the needy, O Lord, be forgotten; *
    Nor the hope of the poor be taken away.
Create in us clean hearts, O God; *
    And sustain us with your Holy Spirit.

For our *brother/sister N.*, let us pray to our Lord Jesus
    Christ who said, "I am Resurrection, and I am
    Life."

Lord, you consoled Martha and Mary in their
    distress; draw near to us who mourn for *N.*, and
    dry the tears of those who weep.

Hear us, Lord.

You wept at the grave of Lazarus, your friend;
    comfort us in our sorrow.

Hear us, Lord.

You raised the dead to life; give to our *brother/sister* eternal life.

Hear us, Lord.

You promised paradise to the thief who repented; bring our *sister/brother* to the joys of heaven.

Hear us, Lord.

Our *brother/sister* was washed in Baptism and anointed with the Holy Spirit; give *him/her* fellowship with all your saints.
Hear us, Lord.

S/he was nourished with your Body and Blood; grant *her/him* a place at the table in your heavenly kingdom.

Hear us, Lord.

Comfort us in our sorrows at the death of *N.;* let our faith be our consolation, and eternal life our hope.†

Silence may follow.

THE COLLECT

Grant, O Lord, to all who are bereaved the spirit of faith and courage, that we may have strength to meet the day to come with steadfastness and patience; not sorrowing without hope, but in remembrance of your great goodness, and in the expectation of eternal life with those we love. And this we ask in the Name of Jesus Christ our Savior. Amen.†

THE MEDITATION

This may be read aloud by one person and followed by silence, or read by all present silently.

Well blest is he who has a dear one dead;
A friend whose face will never change—
A dear communion that will not grow strange;
The anchor of love is death.[5]

JOHN BOYLE O'REILLY

Free intercessions and/or reflections may be offered.

THE REFLECTION

Is there blessing in your loss?
Do you feel your loved one blessing you?

THE CONCLUSION

Let us bless the Lord.
    Thanks be to God.

Keep alert, stand firm in your faith, be courageous, be strong. Let all that you do be done in love. Amen.   1 CORINTHIANS 16:13–14 (NRSV)

MONDAY NOONDAY PRAYER

THE INVITATION TO WORSHIP

Take courage, my children, cry to God. * And he will deliver you from the power and hand of the enemy.

Glory to the Father, and to the Son, and to the Holy Spirit: * as it was in the beginning, is now, and will be for ever. Amen.

PSALM 121

I lift up my eyes to the hills; * from where is my help to come?

My help comes from the LORD, * the maker of heaven and earth.

He will not let your foot be moved * and he who watches over you will not fall asleep.

Behold, he who keeps watch over Israel * shall neither slumber nor sleep;

The LORD himself watches over you; * the LORD is your shade at your right hand,

So that the sun shall not strike you by day, * nor the moon by night.

The LORD shall preserve you from all evil; * it is he who shall keep you safe.

The LORD shall watch over your going out and your coming in, * from this time forth for evermore.

Glory to the Father, and to the Son, and to the Holy Spirit: * as it was in the beginning, is now, and will be for ever. Amen.

THE WORD

Simon Peter asked him, "Lord, where are you going?" Jesus replied, "Where I am going, you cannot follow now, but you will follow later."

JOHN 13:36 (NIV)

Thanks be to God.

THE MEDITATION

This may be read aloud by one person and followed by silence, or read by all present silently.

According to 2 Samuel chapters 12–18, King David fathered many children. One of his sons, Absalom, killed another son, Amnon, because Amnon had raped their sister, Tamar. Absalom went into hiding, and "the soul of King David longed to go forth unto Absalom" (13:39). Still, when David's general Joab tricked the king into allowing Absalom to go home to Jerusalem, "the king said, 'Let him turn to his own house, and let him not see my face.' . . . So Absalom dwelt two full years in Jerusalem, and saw not the king's face" (14:24, 28). Absalom, treating Joab badly in the process, persisted: "Now therefore let me see the king's face; and if there be any iniquity in me, let him kill me. . . . And when he had called for Absalom, he came to the king, and bowed himself on his face to the ground before the king: and the king kissed Absalom" (14:32–33).

Still, Absalom's anger had festered, and he began to plot the overthrow of his father. Charismatic and handsome, with especially beautiful long, thick hair, Absalom was a talented politician. "Absalom said moreover, 'Oh that I were made judge in the land, that every man which hath any suit or cause might come unto me, and I would do him justice!' And it was so, that when any man came nigh to him to do him obeisance, he put forth his hand, and took him, and kissed him. And on this manner did Absalom to all Israel that came to the king for judgment: so Absalom stole the hearts of the men of Israel" (15:4–6).

When the battle between the armies of the king and Absalom the usurper began, David said, "Deal gently for my sake with the young man, even with Absalom. And all the people heard. . . . And Absalom met the servants of David. And Absalom rode upon a mule, and the mule went under the thick boughs of a great oak, and his head caught hold of the oak and he was taken up between the heaven and the earth, and the mule that was under him went away" (18:5, 9).

As Absalom hung by his hair, imprisoned in the oak's branches, Joab drove three spears into the upstart's chest and ordered that the body be flung into a pit and covered with stones.

"And the king was much moved, and went up to the chamber over the gate, and wept: and as he went, thus he said, 'O my son Absalom, my son, my son Absalom! would God I had died for thee, O Absalom, my son, my son!'" (18:33) (KJV).

THE PRAYERS

Lord, have mercy.
    Christ, have mercy.
Lord, have mercy.

Our Father in heaven,
    hallowed be your Name,
    your kingdom come,
    your will be done,
    on earth as in heaven.
Give us today our daily bread.
Forgive us our sins
    as we forgive those
    who sin against us.
Save us from the time of trial,
    and deliver us from evil.

For the kingdom, the power,
    and the glory are yours,
    now and for ever. Amen.

THE COLLECT

O God of grace and glory, *we* remember before
you this day *our* brother (sister) *N. We* thank you
for giving *her/him* to *us*, to know and to love as
a companion on *our* earthly pilgrimage. In your
boundless compassion, console *us* who mourn.
Give *us* faith to see in death the gate of eternal
life, so that in quiet confidence *we* may continue *our* course on earth, until, by your call, *we*
are reunited with those who have gone before;
through Jesus Christ our Lord. Amen.†

Free intercessions and/or reflections may be offered.

THE REFLECTION

In what ways has God responded to you in your loss?
When have you felt God has not responded to your cry?

THE CONCLUSION

Let us bless the Lord.
    Thanks be to God.

Rest eternal grant to *N.*, O Lord,
And let light perpetual shine upon *him/her.*

MONDAY EVENING PRAYER

❧

THE INVITATION TO WORSHIP

I am the Resurrection and I am the Life, says the
  Lord, * Whoever has faith in me shall have life,
  even though he die.
For if we have life, we are alive in the Lord, * And
  if we die, we die in the Lord.
So, then, whether we live or die, * We are the
  Lord's possession.†

O GRACIOUS LIGHT

O gracious Light,
pure brightness of the everliving Father in heaven,
O Jesus Christ, holy and blessed!
Now as we come to the setting of the sun,
and our eyes behold the vesper light,
we sing your praises, O God: Father, Son, and
Holy Spirit.†

PSALM 107:1–9

Give thanks to the LORD, for he is good, * and his
  mercy endures for ever.

Let all those whom the LORD has redeemed
proclaim * that he redeemed them from the
hand of the foe.

He gathered them out of the lands; * from the
east and from the west, from the north and
from the south.

Some wandered in desert wastes; * they found no
way to a city where they might dwell.

They were hungry and thirsty; * their spirits
languished within them.

Then they cried to the LORD in their trouble, *
and he delivered them from their distress.

He put their feet on a straight path * to go to a
city where they might dwell.

Let them give thanks to the LORD for his mercy *
and the wonders he does for his children.

For he satisfies the thirsty * and fills the hungry
with good things.

Glory to the Father, and to the Son, and to the
Holy Spirit: * as it was in the beginning, is now,
and will be for ever. Amen.

THE WORD

For now we see through a glass, darkly:
   but then face to face:
   now I know in part;

but then I shall know
even as also I am known.
                          I CORINTHIANS 13:12 (KJV)

Thanks be to God.

CANTICLE
          THE SONG OF MARY, LUKE 1:46–55

My soul proclaims the greatness of the Lord, my
    spirit rejoices in God my Savior; * for he has
    looked with favor on his lowly servant.

From this day all generations will call me blessed:
    * the Almighty has done great things for me,
    and holy is his Name.

He has mercy on those who fear him * in every
    generation.

He has shown the strength of his arm, * he has
    scattered the proud in their conceit.

He has cast down the mighty from their thrones,
    * and has lifted up the lowly.

He has filled the hungry with good things, * and
    the rich he has sent away empty.

He has come to the help of his servant Israel, * for
    he has remembered his promise of mercy,

The promise he made to our fathers, * to Abraham
    and his children for ever.

Glory to the Father, and to the Son, and to the
    Holy Spirit: * as it was in the beginning, is now,
    and will be for ever. Amen.

THE APOSTLES' CREED

I believe in God, the Father almighty, creator of
heaven and earth.
I believe in Jesus Christ, his only Son, our Lord.
He was conceived by the power of the
Holy Spirit and born of the Virgin Mary.
He suffered under Pontius Pilate, was
crucified, died, and was buried.
He descended to the dead.
On the third day he rose again.
He ascended into heaven, and is seated at
the right hand of the Father.
He will come again to judge the living and
the dead.
I believe in the Holy Spirit, the holy catholic
Church, the communion of saints, the
forgiveness of sins, the resurrection of the
body, and the life everlasting. Amen.

THE PRAYERS

Our Father in heaven,
hallowed be your Name,
your kingdom come,
your will be done,
on earth as in heaven.
Give us today our daily bread.
Forgive us our sins

as we forgive those
    who sin against us.
Save us from the time of trial,
    and deliver us from evil.
For the kingdom, the power,
    and the glory are yours,
    now and for ever. Amen.

THE PETITIONS

Show us your mercy, O Lord; *
    And grant us your salvation.
Clothe your ministers with righteousness; *
    Let your people sing with joy.
Give peace, O Lord, in all the world; *
    For only in you can we live in safety.
Lord, keep this nation under your care; *
    And guide us in the way of justice and truth.
Let your way be known upon earth; *
    Your saving health among all nations.
Let not the needy, O Lord, be forgotten; *
    Nor the hope of the poor be taken away.
Create in us clean hearts, O God; *
    And sustain us with your Holy Spirit.

THE COLLECT

God of all, *we* pray to you for *N.*, and for all those
whom *we* love but see no longer. Grant to them

your peace; let light perpetual shine upon them;
and, in your loving wisdom and almighty power,
work in them the good purpose of your perfect
will, through Jesus Christ our Lord. Amen.†

THE MEDITATION

> *This may be read aloud by one person and followed
> by silence, or read by all present silently.*

What is essential is invisible to the eye.[6]

ANTOINE DE SAINT-EXUPERY

> *Free intercessions and/or reflections may be offered.*

THE REFLECTION

> *How do you "see" those you've lost? How do you think they
> see you from the clearer vantage point of heaven?*

THE CONCLUSION

Let us bless the Lord.
   Thanks be to God.

May the God of hope fill you with all joy and
peace in believing . . . by the power of the Holy
Spirit. Amen.

ROMANS 15:13 (NRSV)

MONDAY COMPLINE

THE INVITATION TO WORSHIP

The Lord Almighty grant us a peaceful night and a perfect end. Amen.

Answer me when I call, O God, defender of my cause; * you set me free when I am hard-pressed; have mercy on me and hear my prayer.

Glory to the Father, and to the Son, and to the Holy Spirit: * as it was in the beginning, is now, and will be for ever. Amen.

PSALM 74:8–22

There are no signs for us to see; there is no prophet left; * there is not one among us who knows how long.

How long, O God, will the adversary scoff? * will the enemy blaspheme your Name for ever?

Why do you draw back your hand? * why is your right hand hidden in your bosom?

Yet God is my King from ancient times, * victorious in the midst of the earth.

You divided the sea by your might * and shattered the heads of the dragons upon the waters;

You crushed the heads of Leviathan * and gave him to the people of the desert for food.

You split open spring and torrent; * you dried up
ever-flowing rivers.

Yours is the day, yours also the night; * you estab-
lished the moon and the sun.

You fixed all the boundaries of the earth; * you
made both summer and winter.

Remember, O LORD, how the enemy scoffed, *
how a foolish people despised your Name.

Do not hand over the life of your dove to wild
beasts; * never forget the lives of your poor.

Look upon your covenant; * the dark places of the
earth are haunts of violence.

Let not the oppressed turn away ashamed; * let the
poor and needy praise your Name.

Arise, O God, maintain your cause; * remember
how fools revile you all day long.

Forget not the clamor of your adversaries, * the
unending tumult of those who rise up against you.

Glory to the Father, and to the Son, and to the
Holy Spirit: * as it was in the beginning, is now,
and will be for ever. Amen.

THE WORD

He reveals the deep things of darkness and brings
deep shadows into the light.

JOB 12:22 (NIV)

Thanks be to God.

THE MEDITATION

*This may be read aloud by one person and followed
by silence, or read by all present silently.*

In You, therefore, O Lord God, I place my whole
hope and refuge; on You I rest in my tribulations
and anguish, for I find all is weak and unstable, no
matter what it is, unless it is in You.

For many friends cannot profit me, nor can
strong helpers assist, nor wise counselors give
profitable answers, nor can the books of the
learned yield any comfort, and no precious
substance can deliver, nor can any place, however
remote and lovely, give shelter, unless You
Yourself assist, help, strengthen, console, instruct,
and guard me.[7]

THOMAS À KEMPIS

THE PRAYERS

Into your hands, O Lord, we commend our
spirits; * For you have redeemed us, O Lord, O
God of truth.

Keep us, O Lord, as the apple of your eye; * Hide
us under the shadow of your wings.†

Lord, have mercy.
Christ, have mercy.
Lord, have mercy.

Our Father in heaven,
  hallowed be your Name,
  your kingdom come,
  your will be done,
  on earth as in heaven.
Give us today our daily bread.
Forgive us our sins
  as we forgive those
  who sin against us.
Save us from the time of trial,
  and deliver us from evil.
For the kingdom, the power,
  and the glory are yours,
  now and for ever. Amen.

Lord, hear our prayer;
  And let our cry come to you.
Let us pray.

Keep watch, dear Lord, with those who work, or watch, or weep this night, and give your angels charge over those who sleep. Tend the sick, Lord Christ; give rest to the weary, bless the dying, soothe the suffering, pity the afflicted, shield the joyous; and all for your love's sake. Amen.

Free intercessions and/or reflections may be offered.

THE REFLECTION

Job's friends gave him unsatisfactory advice, and ultimately he found solace in acknowledging that God is powerful, powerful enough to turn darkness into light. Perhaps Thomas à Kempis had the same experience in the fifteenth century. What helps you discern whether advice is of God? Perhaps using à Kempis's words will help. Take the advice to God and meditate on whether the advice is aiding God in assisting, helping, strengthening, consoling, instructing, and guarding you.

THE CONCLUSION

Lord, you now have set your servant free * to go
   in peace as you have promised;
For these eyes of mine have seen the Savior, *
   whom you have prepared for all the world to see:
A Light to enlighten the nations, * and the glory of
   your people Israel.
Glory to the Father, and to the Son, and to the
   Holy Spirit: * as it was in the beginning, is now,
   and will be for ever. Amen.

Guide us waking, O Lord, and guard us sleeping;
that awake we may watch with Christ, and asleep
we may rest in peace.

Let us bless the Lord.
   Thanks be to God.

The almighty and merciful Lord, Father, Son, and Holy Spirit, bless us and keep us. Amen.

THOUGHTS & MEMORIES

TUESDAY

TUESDAY MORNING PRAYER

THE INVITATION TO WORSHIP

Out of the deep have I called unto thee, O Lord: *
Lord, hear my voice.

The Lord is full of compassion and mercy: *
Come, let us adore him.

Glory to the Father, and to the Son, and to the
Holy Spirit: * as it was in the beginning, is now,
and will be for ever. Amen.

PSALM 61:1–5

Hear my cry, O God, * and listen to my prayer.

I call upon you from the ends of the earth with
heaviness in my heart; * set me upon the rock
that is higher than I.

For you have been my refuge, * a strong tower
against the enemy.

I will dwell in your house for ever; * I will take
refuge under the cover of your wings.

For you, O God, have heard my vows; * you
have granted me the heritage of those who
fear your Name.

Glory to the Father, and to the Son, and to the
Holy Spirit: * as it was in the beginning, is now,
and will be for ever. Amen.

THE WORD

"Do not let your hearts be troubled.
You trust in God, trust also in me.
In my Father's house there are many places to
live in; otherwise I would have told you.
I am going now to prepare a place for you,
and after I have gone and prepared you a place,
I shall return to take you to myself,
so that you may be with me where I am."

JOHN 14:1–3 (NJB)

Thanks be to God.

CANTICLE
THE THIRD SONG OF ISAIAH, ISAIAH 60:1–3, 11A, 14C, 18–19

Arise, shine, for your light has come, * and the
glory of the Lord has dawned upon you.
For behold, darkness covers the land; * deep
gloom enshrouds the peoples.
But over you the Lord will rise, * and his glory will
appear upon you.
Nations will stream to your light, * and kings to
the brightness of your dawning.
Your gates will always be open; * by day or night
they will never be shut.
They will call you The City of the Lord, * The
Zion of the Holy One of Israel.
Violence will no more be heard in your land, *
ruin or destruction within your borders.

You will call your walls, Salvation, * and all your
   portals, Praise.
The sun will no more be your light by day; * by
   night you will not need the brightness of the
   moon.
The Lord will be your everlasting light, * and your
   God will be your glory.
Glory to the Father, and to the Son, and to the
   Holy Spirit: * as it was in the beginning, is now,
   and will be for ever. Amen.

THE APOSTLES' CREED

I believe in God, the Father almighty, creator of
   heaven and earth.
I believe in Jesus Christ, his only Son, our Lord.
   He was conceived by the power of the
   Holy Spirit and born of the Virgin Mary.
   He suffered under Pontius Pilate, was
   crucified, died, and was buried.
   He descended to the dead.
   On the third day he rose again.
   He ascended into heaven, and is seated at
   the right hand of the Father.
   He will come again to judge the living and
   the dead.
I believe in the Holy Spirit, the holy catholic
   Church, the communion of saints, the

forgiveness of sins, the resurrection of the
body, and the life everlasting. Amen.

THE PRAYERS

Our Father in heaven,
  hallowed be your Name,
  your kingdom come,
  your will be done,
  on earth as in heaven.
Give us today our daily bread.
Forgive us our sins
  as we forgive those
  who sin against us.
Save us from the time of trial,
  and deliver us from evil.
For the kingdom, the power,
  and the glory are yours,
  now and for ever. Amen.

THE PETITIONS

Save your people, Lord, and bless your inheritance;
  * Govern and uphold them, now and always.
Day by day we bless you; * We praise your Name
  for ever.
Lord, keep us from all sin today; * Have mercy on
  us; Lord, have mercy.

Lord, show us your love and mercy; * For we put our trust in you.

In you, Lord, is our hope; * And we shall never hope in vain.

For our *brother/sister N.*, let us pray to our Lord Jesus Christ who said, "I am Resurrection, and I am Life."

Lord, you consoled Martha and Mary in their distress; draw near to us who mourn for *N.*, and dry the tears of those who weep.

Hear us, Lord.

You wept at the grave of Lazarus, your friend; comfort us in our sorrow.

Hear us, Lord.

You raised the dead to life; give to our *brother/sister* eternal life.

Hear us, Lord.

You promised paradise to the thief who repented; bring our *sister/brother* to the joys of heaven.

Hear us, Lord.

Our *brother/sister* was washed in Baptism and anointed with the Holy Spirit; give *him/her* fellowship with all your saints.

Hear us, Lord.

S/he was nourished with your Body and Blood; grant *her/him* a place at the table in your heavenly kingdom.

Hear us, Lord.

Comfort us in our sorrows at the death of *N.*; let our faith be our consolation, and eternal life our hope.†

Silence may follow.

THE COLLECT

Grant, O Lord, to all who are bereaved the spirit of faith and courage, that *we* may have strength to meet the day to come with steadfastness and patience; not sorrowing without hope, but in remembrance of your great goodness, and in the expectation of eternal life with those *we* love. And this *we* ask in the Name of Jesus Christ our Savior. Amen.†

THE MEDITATION

This may be read aloud by one person and followed by silence, or read by all present silently.

These words: You will not be overcome, were said very insistently and strongly [by Jesus], for certainty and strength against every tribulation which may come. He did not say, "You will not be assailed, you will not be belabored, you will not be disquieted," but he said, "You will not be overcome."[8]   JULIAN OF NORWICH

Free intercessions and/or reflections may be offered.

THE REFLECTION

At the age of 30½, Julian of Norwich was thought to be on her deathbed. In actuality, she was experiencing some of the most vivid visions of the suffering and risen Christ ever recorded. Julian received her visions while the plague, or Black Death, was striking down many people in its vicious path. Her visions, which gave her courage to live in conversation with God, included the image of God as close as our clothing and the image of God's love as common as the hazelnuts that carpeted the part of England where she lived.

This morning's psalm and Gospel speak of God and Jesus preparing homes for us, on earth and in heaven.

What kinds of images has your suffering brought? Have your images of God and images of your relationship with God changed in your grief?

THE CONCLUSION

Let us bless the Lord.
    Thanks be to God.

Keep alert, stand firm in your faith, be courageous, be strong. Let all that you do be done in love. Amen.   1 CORINTHIANS 16:13–14 (NRSV)

TUESDAY NOONDAY
PRAYER

THE INVITATION TO WORSHIP

Take courage, my children, cry to God. * And he
will deliver you from the power and hand of
the enemy.

Glory to the Father, and to the Son, and to the
Holy Spirit: * as it was in the beginning, is now,
and will be for ever. Amen.

PSALM 42

As the deer longs for the water-brooks, * so
longs my soul for you, O God.

My soul is athirst for God, athirst for the living
God; * when shall I come to appear before the
presence of God?

My tears have been my food day and night, *
while all day long they say to me, "Where
now is your God?"

I pour out my soul when I think on these things:
* how I went with the multitude and led them
into the house of God,

With the voice of praise and thanksgiving, *
among those who keep holy-day.

Why are you so full of heaviness, O my soul? *
and why are you so disquieted within me?

Put your trust in God; * for I will yet give thanks
to him, who is the help of my countenance,
and my God.

My soul is heavy within me; * therefore I will
remember you from the land of Jordan, and
from the peak of Mizar among the heights of
Hermon.

One deep calls to another in the noise of your
cataracts; * all your rapids and floods have
gone over me.

The Lord grants his loving-kindness in the daytime; * in the night season his song is with me,
a prayer to the God of my life.

I will say to the God of my strength, "Why
have you forgotten me? * and why do I go so
heavily while the enemy oppresses me?"

While my bones are being broken, * my enemies
mock me to my face;

All day long they mock me * and say to me,
"Where now is your God?"

Why are you so full of heaviness, O my soul? *
and why are you so disquieted within me?

Put your trust in God; * for I will yet give thanks
to him, who is the help of my countenance, and
my God.

Glory to the Father, and to the Son, and to the
    Holy Spirit: * as it was in the beginning, is now,
    and will be for ever. Amen.

THE WORD

The LORD is good to those whose hope is in
    him, to the one who seeks him; it is good to wait
    quietly for the salvation of the LORD.

LAMENTATIONS 3:25–26 (NIV)

Thanks be to God.

THE MEDITATION

*This may be read aloud by one person and followed
    by silence, or read by all present silently.*

Nothing can make up for the absence of someone
whom we love, and it would be wrong to try to
find a substitute; we must simply hold out and
see it through. That sounds very hard at first, but
at the same time it is a great consolation, for the
gap, as long as it remains unfilled, preserves the
bonds between us. It is nonsense to say that God
fills the gap; He doesn't fill it, but on the contrary,
He keeps it empty and so helps us to keep alive
our former communion with each other, even at
the cost of pain.[9]

DIETRICH BONHOEFFER

THE PRAYERS

Lord, have mercy.
  Christ, have mercy.
Lord, have mercy.

Our Father in heaven,
  hallowed be your Name,
  your kingdom come,
  your will be done,
  on earth as in heaven.
Give us today our daily bread.
Forgive us our sins
  as we forgive those
  who sin against us.
Save us from the time of trial,
  and deliver us from evil.
For the kingdom, the power,
  and the glory are yours,
  now and for ever. Amen.

THE COLLECT

O God of grace and glory, *we* remember before you this day *our* brother (sister) *N. We* thank you for giving *her/him* to *us*, to know and to love as a companion on *our* earthly pilgrimage. In your boundless compassion, console *us* who mourn. Give *us* faith to see in death the gate of eternal life, so that in quiet confidence *we* may

continue *our* course on earth, until, by your call,
we are reunited with those who have gone before;
through Jesus Christ our Lord. Amen.†

Free intercessions and/or reflections may be offered.

THE REFLECTION

*Do you feel a "gap" between you and your loved one?
Describe it to your loved one—and to God. Do you think
your loved one feels a gap? If so, how do you imagine the gap
feels to your loved one?*

THE CONCLUSION

Let us bless the Lord.
   Thanks be to God.

Rest eternal grant to *N.*, O Lord,
And let light perpetual shine upon *him/her.*

TUESDAY EVENING
PRAYER

THE INVITATION TO WORSHIP

I am the Resurrection and I am the Life, says the
   Lord, * Whoever has faith in me shall have life,
   even though he die.

For if we have life, we are alive in the Lord, * And
if we die, we die in the Lord.
So, then, whether we live or die, * We are the
Lord's possession.†

O GRACIOUS LIGHT

O gracious Light,
pure brightness of the everliving Father in heaven,
O Jesus Christ, holy and blessed!
Now as we come to the setting of the sun,
and our eyes behold the vesper light,
we sing your praises, O God: Father, Son, and
Holy Spirit.†

PSALM 27:1, 5–13, 17–18

The LORD is my light and my salvation; whom
then shall I fear? * the LORD is the strength of
my life; of whom then shall I be afraid?
One thing have I asked of the LORD; one thing
I seek; * that I may dwell in the house of the
LORD all the days of my life;
To behold the fair beauty of the LORD * and to
seek him in his temple.
For in the day of trouble he shall keep me safe in
his shelter; * he shall hide me in the secrecy of
his dwelling and set me high upon a rock.

Even now he lifts up my head * above my enemies
round about me.

Therefore I will offer in his dwelling an oblation
with sounds of great gladness; * I will sing and
make music to the LORD.

Hearken to my voice, O LORD, when I call; * have
mercy on me and answer me.

You speak in my heart and say, "Seek my face." *
Your face, LORD, will I seek.

Hide not your face from me, * nor turn away your
servant in displeasure.

You have been my helper; cast me not away; * do
not forsake me, O God of my salvation.

What if I had not believed that I should see the
goodness of the LORD * in the land of the living!

O tarry and await the LORD's pleasure; be strong,
and he shall comfort your heart; * wait patiently
for the LORD.

Glory to the Father, and to the Son, and to the
Holy Spirit: * as it was in the beginning, is now,
and will be for ever. Amen.

THE WORD

Trust in the LORD forever, * for the LORD,
the LORD, is the Rock eternal.

ISAIAH 26:4 (NIV)

Thanks be to God.

CANTICLE
THE SONG OF MARY, LUKE 1:46–55

My soul proclaims the greatness of the LORD, my
spirit rejoices in God my Savior; * for he has
looked with favor on his lowly servant.

From this day all generations will call me blessed:
* the Almighty has done great things for me,
and holy is his Name.

He has mercy on those who fear him * in every
generation.

He has shown the strength of his arm, * he has
scattered the proud in their conceit.

He has cast down the mighty from their thrones,
* and has lifted up the lowly.

He has filled the hungry with good things, * and
the rich he has sent away empty.

He has come to the help of his servant Israel, * for
he has remembered his promise of mercy,

The promise he made to our fathers, * to Abraham
and his children for ever.

Glory to the Father, and to the Son, and to the
Holy Spirit: * as it was in the beginning, is now,
and will be for ever. Amen.

THE APOSTLES' CREED

I believe in God, the Father almighty, creator of
heaven and earth.

I believe in Jesus Christ, his only Son, our Lord.
 He was conceived by the power of the
 Holy Spirit and born of the Virgin Mary.
 He suffered under Pontius Pilate, was
 crucified, died, and was buried.
 He descended to the dead.
 On the third day he rose again.
 He ascended into heaven, and is seated at
 the right hand of the Father.
 He will come again to judge the living and
 the dead.
I believe in the Holy Spirit, the holy catholic
 Church, the communion of saints, the
 forgiveness of sins, the resurrection of the
 body, and the life everlasting. Amen.

THE PRAYERS

Our Father in heaven,
 hallowed be your Name,
 your kingdom come,
 your will be done,
 on earth as in heaven.
Give us today our daily bread.
Forgive us our sins
 as we forgive those
 who sin against us.
Save us from the time of trial,
 and deliver us from evil.

For the kingdom, the power,
   and the glory are yours,
   now and for ever. Amen.

THE PETITIONS

Show us your mercy, O Lord; *
   And grant us your salvation.
Clothe your ministers with righteousness; *
   Let your people sing with joy.
Give peace, O Lord, in all the world; *
   For only in you can we live in safety.
Lord, keep this nation under your care; *
   And guide us in the way of justice and truth.
Let your way be known upon earth; *
   Your saving health among all nations.
Let not the needy, O Lord, be forgotten; *
   Nor the hope of the poor be taken away.
Create in us clean hearts, O God; *
   And sustain us with your Holy Spirit.

THE COLLECT

God of all, *we* pray to you for *N.*, and for all those
whom *we* love but see no longer. Grant to them
your peace; let light perpetual shine upon them;
and, in your loving wisdom and almighty power,
work in them the good purpose of your perfect
will, through Christ our Lord. Amen.†

THE MEDITATION

*This may be read aloud by one person and followed
by silence, or read by all present silently.*

"Listen to the Right Voice."

Jesus Christ is the One we must listen to. As far as
people are concerned, we ought to listen to them and
believe them only insomuch as they are full of Jesus
Christ's truth and authority. Books are good only to
the extent that they teach us the good news of the
gospel. Therefore, let us go straight to that sacred
source.[10]   FRANÇOIS FÉNELON

Free intercessions and/or reflections may be offered.

THE REFLECTION

*Perhaps you find yourself receiving all kinds of advice, and
wondering what of it to take and what of it to leave. This
evening's psalm and Scripture give us the images of God as light
and as a rock—very different images! What images of God help
you turn to God as you discern advice you're given?*

THE CONCLUSION

Let us bless the Lord.
    Thanks be to God.

May the God of hope fill you with all joy and
peace in believing . . . by the power of the Holy
Spirit. Amen.   ROMANS 15:13 (NRSV)

TUESDAY COMPLINE

THE INVITATION TO WORSHIP

The Lord Almighty grant us a peaceful night and a perfect end. Amen.

Answer me when I call, O God, defender of my cause; * you set me free when I am hard-pressed; have mercy on me and hear my prayer.

Glory to the Father, and to the Son, and to the Holy Spirit: * as it was in the beginning, is now, and will be for ever. Amen.

PSALM 18:1–4, 6–7, 10–20

I love you, O LORD my strength, * O LORD my stronghold, my crag, and my haven.

My God, my rock in whom I put my trust, * my shield, the horn of my salvation, and my refuge; you are worthy of praise.

I will call upon the LORD, * and so shall I be saved from my enemies.

The breakers of death rolled over me, * and the torrents of oblivion made me afraid.

I called upon the LORD in my distress * and cried out to my God for help.

He heard my voice from his heavenly dwelling; * my cry of anguish came to his ears.

He parted the heavens and came down * with a storm cloud under his feet.

He mounted on cherubim and flew; * he swooped on the wings of the wind.

He wrapped darkness about him; * he made dark waters and thick clouds his pavilion.

From the brightness of his presence, through the clouds, * burst hailstones and coals of fire.

The LORD thundered out of heaven; * the Most High uttered his voice.

He loosed his arrows and scattered them; * he hurled thunderbolts and routed them.

The beds of the seas were uncovered, and the foundations of the world laid bare, * at your battle cry, O LORD, at the blast of the breath of your nostrils.

He reached down from on high and grasped me; * he drew me out of great waters.

He delivered me from my strong enemies and from those who hated me; * for they were too mighty for me.

They confronted me in the day of my disaster; * but the LORD was my support.

He brought me out into an open place; * he rescued me because he delighted in me.

Glory to the Father, and to the Son, and to the Holy Spirit: * as it was in the beginning, is now, and will be for ever. Amen.

THE WORD

Who shall separate us from the love of Christ?
Neither death, nor life, nor angels, nor
    principalities, nor powers, nor things present,
    nor things to come,
Nor height, nor depth, nor any other creature,
    shall be able to separate us from the love of
    God, which is in Christ our Lord.

ROMANS 8:35, 38–39 (KJV)

Thanks be to God.

THE MEDITATION

*This may be read aloud by one person and followed
by silence, or read by all present silently.*

Love is little
    Love is low.
Love will make
    My spirit grow.
Grow in peace,
    Grow in light,
Love will do
    The thing that's right.

TRADITIONAL SHAKER HYMN

THE PRAYERS

Into your hands, O Lord, we commend our
spirits; * For you have redeemed us, O Lord,
O God of truth.
Keep us, O Lord, as the apple of your eye; *
Hide us under the shadow of your wings.†

Lord, have mercy.
Christ, have mercy.
Lord, have mercy.

Our Father in heaven,
hallowed be your Name,
your kingdom come,
your will be done,
on earth as in heaven.
Give us today our daily bread.
Forgive us our sins
as we forgive those
who sin against us.
Save us from the time of trial,
and deliver us from evil.
For the kingdom, the power,
and the glory are yours,
now and for ever. Amen.

Lord, hear our prayer;
And let our cry come to you.
Let us pray.

Keep watch, dear Lord, with those who work, or watch, or weep this night, and give your angels charge over those who sleep. Tend the sick, Lord Christ; give rest to the weary, bless the dying, soothe the suffering, pity the afflicted, shield the joyous; and all for your love's sake. Amen.

Free intercessions and/or reflections may be offered.

THE REFLECTION

According to Paul, love is strong, yet the Shaker hymn describes love as gentle. And the psalmist portrays God loving through righteous anger. What is your grief teaching you about love?

THE CONCLUSION

Lord, you now have set your servant free * to go in peace as you have promised;

For these eyes of mine have seen the Savior, * whom you have prepared for all the world to see:

A Light to enlighten the nations, * and the glory of your people Israel.

Glory to the Father, and to the Son, and to the Holy Spirit: * as it was in the beginning, is now, and will be forever. Amen.

Guide us waking, O Lord, and guard us sleeping; that awake we may watch with Christ, and asleep we may rest in peace.

Let us bless the Lord.
  Thanks be to God.

The almighty and merciful Lord, Father, Son, and
Holy Spirit, bless us and keep us.

THOUGHTS & MEMORIES

WEDNESDAY

WEDNESDAY MORNING PRAYER

THE INVITATION TO WORSHIP

Out of the deep have I called unto thee, O Lord: *
Lord, hear my voice.

The Lord is full of compassion and mercy: *
Come, let us adore him.

Glory to the Father, and to the Son, and to the
Holy Spirit: * as it was in the beginning, is now,
and will be for ever. Amen.

PSALM 46

God is our refuge and strength, * a very present
help in trouble.

Therefore we will not fear, though the earth be
moved, * and though the mountains be toppled
into the depths of the sea;

Though its waters rage and foam, * and though
the mountains tremble at its tumult.

The LORD of hosts is with us; * the God of Jacob
is our stronghold.

There is a river whose streams make glad the city
of God, * the holy habitation of the Most High.

God is in the midst of her; she shall not be over-
   thrown; * God shall help her at the break of day.
The nations make much ado, and the kingdoms
   are shaken; * God has spoken, and the earth
   shall melt away.
The LORD of hosts is with us; * the God of Jacob
   is our stronghold.
Come now and look upon the works of the LORD,
   * what awesome things he has done on earth.
It is he who makes war to cease in all the world; *
   he breaks the bow, and shatters the spear, and
   burns the shields with fire.
"Be still, then, and know that I am God; * I will be
   exalted among the nations; I will be exalted in
   the earth."
The LORD of hosts is with us; * the God of Jacob
   is our stronghold.
Glory to the Father, and to the Son, and to the
   Holy Spirit: * as it was in the beginning, is now,
   and will be for ever. Amen.

THE WORD

On this mountain the LORD Almighty will prepare
a feast of rich food for all peoples, a banquet of
aged wine—
the best of meats and the finest of wines.
On this mountain he will destroy

the shroud that enfolds all peoples,
the sheet that covers all nations;
he will swallow up death forever.

The Sovereign LORD will wipe away the tears
from all faces;
he will remove the disgrace of his people
from all the earth.
The LORD has spoken.

In that day they will say,
"Surely this is our God;
we trusted in him, and he saved us.

This is the LORD, we trusted in him;
let us rejoice and be glad in his salvation."

ISAIAH 25:6–9 (NIV)

Thanks be to God.

CANTICLE
PRAYER OF MANASSEH, 1–2, 4, 6–7, 14

O Lord and Ruler of the hosts of heaven, * God
of Abraham, Isaac, and Jacob, and of all their
righteous offspring:
You made the heavens and the earth, * with all
their vast array.
All things quake with fear at your presence; * they
tremble because of your power.
But your merciful promise is beyond all measure; *
it surpasses all that our minds can fathom.

O Lord, you are full of compassion, * long-
suffering, and abounding in mercy.

You will save me in accordance with your great
mercy. Amen.

Glory to the Father, and to the Son, and to the
Holy Spirit: * as it was in the beginning, is now,
and will be for ever. Amen.

THE APOSTLES' CREED

I believe in God, the Father almighty, creator of
heaven and earth.

I believe in Jesus Christ, his only Son, our Lord.
He was conceived by the power of the
Holy Spirit and born of the Virgin Mary.
He suffered under Pontius Pilate, was
crucified, died, and was buried.
He descended to the dead.
On the third day he rose again.
He ascended into heaven, and is seated at
the right hand of the Father.
He will come again to judge the living and
the dead.

I believe in the Holy Spirit, the holy catholic
Church, the communion of saints, the
forgiveness of sins, the resurrection of the
body, and the life everlasting. Amen.

THE PRAYERS

Our Father in heaven,
    hallowed be your Name,
    your kingdom come,
    your will be done,
    on earth as in heaven.
Give us today our daily bread.
Forgive us our sins
    as we forgive those
    who sin against us.
Save us from the time of trial,
    and deliver us from evil.
For the kingdom, the power,
    and the glory are yours,
    now and for ever. Amen.

THE PETITIONS

Show us your mercy, O Lord; *
    And grant us your salvation.
Clothe your ministers with righteousness; *
    Let your people sing with joy.
Give peace, O Lord, in all the world; *
    For only in you can we live in safety.
Lord, keep this nation under your care; *
    And guide us in the way of justice and truth.
Let your way be known upon earth; *
    Your saving health among all nations.

Let not the needy, O Lord, be forgotten; *
  Nor the hope of the poor be taken away.
Create in us clean hearts, O God; *

For our *brother/sister N.*, let us pray to our Lord Jesus
  Christ who said, "I am Resurrection, and I am
  Life."

Lord, you consoled Martha and Mary in their
  distress; draw near to us who mourn for *N.*, and
  dry the tears of those who weep.

Hear us, Lord.
You wept at the grave of Lazarus, your friend;
  comfort us in our sorrow.

Hear us, Lord.

You raised the dead to life; give to our *brother/sister*
  eternal life.

Hear us, Lord.

You promised paradise to the thief who repented;
  bring our *sister/brother* to the joys of heaven.

Hear us, Lord.

Our *brother/sister* was washed in Baptism and anointed
  with the Holy Spirit; give *him/her* fellowship with
  all your saints.

Hear us, Lord.

S/he was nourished with your Body and Blood; grant *her/him* a place at the table in your heavenly kingdom.

Hear us, Lord.

Comfort us in our sorrows at the death of *N.*; let our faith be our consolation, and eternal life our hope.†

Silence may follow.

THE COLLECT

Grant, O Lord, to all who are bereaved the spirit of faith and courage, that *we* may have strength to meet the day to come with steadfastness and patience; not sorrowing without hope, but in remembrance of your great goodness, and in the expectation of eternal life with those *we* love. And this *we* ask in the Name of Jesus Christ our Savior. Amen.†

THE MEDITATION

This may be read aloud by one person and followed by silence, or read by all present silently.

"O Grief"

O who will give me tears? Come all you springs, Dwell in my head and eyes; come clouds and rain:

My grief needs all the watery things
That nature has produced. Let every vein
Suck up a river to supply my eyes,
My weary weeping eyes too dry for me,
Unless they get new conduits, new supplies
To bear them out, and with my state agree.
What are two shallow fords, two little spouts
Of a less world? The greater is but small,
A narrow cupboard for my griefs and doubts,
Which lack provision in the midst of all.
Verses, you are too fine a thing, too wise
For my rough sorrows; cease, be dumb and mute,
Give up your feet and running to my eyes,
And keep your measures for some lover's lute,
Whose grief allows him music and a rhyme:
For mine excludes both measure, tune, and time.
Alas, my God![11]

GEORGE HERBERT

Free intercessions and/or reflections may be offered.

THE REFLECTION

*What do your tears mean? What purposes do your tears
have? What do you think about the tears of Jesus, who
wept when he was told Lazarus was dead?*

THE CONCLUSION

Let us bless the Lord.
Thanks be to God.

Keep alert, stand firm in your faith, be courageous, be strong. Let all that you do be done in
love. Amen.   1 CORINTHIANS 16:13–14 (NRSV)

WEDNESDAY NOONDAY PRAYER

THE INVITATION TO WORSHIP

Take courage, my children, cry to God. * And he
will deliver you from the power and hand of
the enemy.
Glory to the Father, and to the Son, and to the
Holy Spirit: * as it was in the beginning, is now,
and will be for ever. Amen.

PSALM 119:169–176

Let my cry come before you, O LORD; * give me
understanding, according to your word.
Let my supplication come before you; * deliver
me, according to your promise.

My lips shall pour forth your praise, * when you
    teach me your statutes.
My tongue shall sing of your promise, * for all
    your commandments are righteous.
Let your hand be ready to help me, * for I have
    chosen your commandments.
I long for your salvation, O LORD, * and your law
    is my delight.
Let me live, and I will praise you, * and let your
    judgments help me.
I have gone astray like a sheep that is lost; * search
    for your servant, for I do not forget your com-
    mandments.
Glory to the Father, and to the Son, and to the
    Holy Spirit: * as it was in the beginning, is now,
    and will be for ever. Amen.

THE WORD

There is always hope for a tree:
when felled, it can start its life again;
its shoots continue to sprout.

Its roots may have grown old in the earth,
its stump rotting in the ground,
but let it scent the water, and it buds,
and puts out branches like a plant newly set.

Can the dead come back to life?

Day after day of my service, I should be waiting for my relief to come.

Then you would call, and I should answer, you would want to see once more what you have made.   JOB 14:7–9, 14–15 (NJB)

Thanks be to God.

THE MEDITATION

This may be read aloud by one person and followed
by silence, or read by all present silently.

Oh, only for so short a while have you loaned us to each other, because we take form in your act of drawing us, and we take life in your painting us, and we breathe in your singing us. But only for so short a while have you loaned us to each other.

TRADITIONAL AZTEC PRAYER

THE PRAYERS

Lord, have mercy.
    Christ, have mercy.
Lord, have mercy.

Our Father in heaven,
    hallowed be your Name,
    your kingdom come,
    your will be done,
    on earth as in heaven.

Give us today our daily bread.
Forgive us our sins
   as we forgive those
   who sin against us.
Save us from the time of trial,
   and deliver us from evil.
For the kingdom, the power,
   and the glory are yours,
   now and for ever. Amen.

THE COLLECT

O God of grace and glory, *we* remember before you this day *our* brother (sister) N. *We* thank you for giving *her/him* to *us*, to know and to love as a companion on *our* earthly pilgrimage. In your boundless compassion, console *us* who mourn. Give *us* faith to see in death the gate of eternal life, so that in quiet confidence *we* may continue our course on earth, until, by your call, *we* are reunited with those who have gone before; through Jesus Christ our Lord. Amen.†

Free intercessions and/or reflections may be offered.

THE REFLECTION

This noon's Scripture is from Job's "despondent prayer." Later, he proclaims, "I know that my redeemer liveth, and that he shall stand at the latter day upon the earth: And though after my skin worms destroy this body, yet in my flesh shall I see God" (19:25–26, KJV). *How do you think his outlook was transformed? In what ways are you changing in the midst of your suffering?*

THE CONCLUSION

Let us bless the Lord.
　　Thanks be to God.

Rest eternal grant to *N.*, O Lord,
And let light perpetual shine upon *him/her.*

WEDNESDAY EVENING PRAYER

THE INVITATION TO WORSHIP

I am the Resurrection and I am the Life, says the
　　Lord, * Whoever has faith in me shall have life,
　　even though he die.
For if we have life, we are alive in the Lord, * And
　　if we die, we die in the Lord.
So, then, whether we live or die, * We are the
　　Lord's possession.†

O GRACIOUS LIGHT

O gracious Light,
pure brightness of the everliving Father in heaven,
O Jesus Christ, holy and blessed!
Now as we come to the setting of the sun,
and our eyes behold the vesper light,
we sing your praises, O God: Father, Son,
and Holy Spirit.†

PSALM 116:1–15

I love the LORD, because he has heard the voice of
    my supplication, * because he has inclined his
    ear to me whenever I called upon him.

The cords of death entangled me; the grip of the
    grave took hold of me; * I came to grief and sorrow.

Then I called upon the Name of the LORD: * "O
    LORD, I pray you, save my life."

Gracious is the LORD and righteous; * our God is
    full of compassion.

The LORD watches over the innocent; * I was
    brought very low, and he helped me.

Turn again to your rest, O my soul, * for the LORD
    has treated you well.

For you have rescued my life from death, * my
    eyes from tears, and my feet from stumbling.

I will walk in the presence of the LORD * in the
    land of the living.

I believed, even when I said, "I have been brought
very low." * In my distress I said, "No one can
be trusted."

How shall I repay the LORD * for all the good
things he has done for me?

I will lift up the cup of salvation * and call upon
the Name of the LORD.

I will fulfill my vows to the LORD * in the presence
of all his people.

Precious in the sight of the LORD * is the death of
his servants.

O LORD, I am your servant; * I am your servant
and the child of your handmaid; you have freed
me from my bonds.

I will offer you the sacrifice of thanksgiving * and
call upon the Name of the LORD.

Glory to the Father, and to the Son, and to the
Holy Spirit: * as it was in the beginning, is now,
and will be for ever. Amen.

THE WORD

"Come to me, all you who labor and are
overburdened, and I will give you rest.

Shoulder my yoke and learn from me, for I am
gentle and humble in heart, and you will find
rest for your souls.

Yes, my yoke is easy, and my burden light."

MATTHEW 11:28–30 (NJB)

Thanks be to God.

CANTICLE
THE SONG OF MARY, LUKE 1:46–55

My soul proclaims the greatness of the Lord, my spirit rejoices in God my Savior; * for he has looked with favor on his lowly servant.

From this day all generations will call me blessed: * the Almighty has done great things for me, and holy is his Name.

He has mercy on those who fear him * in every generation.

He has shown the strength of his arm, * he has scattered the proud in their conceit.

He has cast down the mighty from their thrones, * and has lifted up the lowly.

He has filled the hungry with good things, * and the rich he has sent away empty.

He has come to the help of his servant Israel, * for he has remembered his promise of mercy,

The promise he made to our fathers, * to Abraham and his children for ever.

Glory to the Father, and to the Son, and to the Holy Spirit: * as it was in the beginning, is now, and will be for ever. Amen.

THE APOSTLES' CREED

I believe in God, the Father almighty, creator of
heaven and earth.

I believe in Jesus Christ, his only Son, our Lord.
He was conceived by the power of the
Holy Spirit and born of the Virgin Mary.
He suffered under Pontius Pilate, was
crucified, died, and was buried.
He descended to the dead.
On the third day he rose again.
He ascended into heaven, and is seated at
the right hand of the Father.
He will come again to judge the living and
the dead.

I believe in the Holy Spirit, the holy catholic
Church, the communion of saints, the
forgiveness of sins, the resurrection of the
body, and the life everlasting. Amen.

THE PRAYERS

Our Father in heaven,
hallowed be your Name,
your kingdom come,
your will be done,
on earth as in heaven.
Give us today our daily bread.

Forgive us our sins
    as we forgive those
    who sin against us.
Save us from the time of trial,
    and deliver us from evil.
For the kingdom, the power,
    and the glory are yours,
    now and for ever. Amen.

THE PETITION

Show us your mercy, O Lord; *
    And grant us your salvation.
Clothe your ministers with righteousness; *
    Let your people sing with joy.
Give peace, O Lord, in all the world; *
    For only in you can we live in safety.
Lord, keep this nation under your care; *
    And guide us in the way of justice and truth.
Let your way be known upon earth; *
    Your saving health among all nations.
Let not the needy, O Lord, be forgotten; *
    Nor the hope of the poor be taken away.
Create in us clean hearts, O God; *
    And sustain us with your Holy Spirit.

THE COLLECT

God of all, *we* pray to you for *N.*, and for all those whom *we* love but see no longer. Grant to them your peace; let light perpetual shine upon them; and, in your loving wisdom and almighty power, work in them the good purpose of your perfect will, through Christ our Lord. Amen.†

THE MEDITATION

This may be read aloud by one person and followed by silence, or read by all present silently.

The practice of the presence of God strengthens our hope. Our hope increases as our spiritual knowledge increases, as our faith lays hold the very secrets of God. By finding in God a beauty surpassing not only physical bodies on earth, but the beauty of the most perfect souls and of angels, our hope is strengthened.[12]

BROTHER LAWRENCE

Free intercessions and/or reflections may be offered.

THE REFLECTION

Do you find obstacles when you try to rest in God? What does your hesitation tell you—and God? Do you think that practicing hope will help you grow in God? One way of practicing hope may be psalms such as tonight's, in which the psalmist is looking back at a hopeless time of grief and sorrow.

THE CONCLUSION

Let us bless the Lord.
　Thanks be to God.

May the God of hope fill you with all joy and peace in believing . . . by the power of the Holy Spirit. Amen.

ROMANS 15:13 (NRSV)

WEDNESDAY COMPLINE

THE INVITATION TO WORSHIP

The Lord Almighty grant us a peaceful night and a perfect end. Amen.

Answer me when I call, O God, defender of my cause; * you set me free when I am hard-pressed; have mercy on me and hear my prayer.
Glory to the Father, and to the Son, and to the Holy Spirit: * as it was in the beginning, is now, and will be for ever. Amen.

PSALM 146:4–9

Happy are they who have the God of Jacob for their
help! * whose hope is in the LORD their God;

Who made heaven and earth, the seas, and all that
is in them; * who keeps his promise for ever;

Who gives justice to those who are oppressed, *
and food to those who hunger.

The LORD sets the prisoners free; the LORD opens
the eyes of the blind; * the LORD lifts up those
who are bowed down;

The LORD loves the righteous; the LORD cares
for the stranger; * he sustains the orphan and
widow, but frustrates the way of the wicked.

The LORD shall reign for ever, * your God, O
Zion, throughout all generations.

Glory to the Father, and to the Son, and to the
Holy Spirit: * as it was in the beginning, is now,
and will be for ever. Amen.

THE WORD

Jacob left Beersheba and set out for Haran. When
he reached a certain place, he stopped for the night
because the sun had set. Taking one of the stones
there, he put it under his head and lay down to sleep.

He had a dream in which he saw a stairway
resting on the earth, with its top reaching to

heaven, and the angels of God were ascending and descending on it.

There above it stood the LORD, and he said, "I am the LORD, the God of your father Abraham and the God of Isaac. . . . I am with you and will watch over you wherever you go, and I will bring you back to this land. I will not leave you until I have done what I have promised you."

When Jacob awoke from his sleep, he thought, "Surely the LORD is in this place and I was not aware of it." He was afraid and said, "How awesome is this place! This is none other than the house of God; this is the gate of heaven."

GENESIS 28:10–13, 15–17 (NRSV)

Thanks be to God.

THE MEDITATION

This may be read aloud by one person and followed by silence, or read by all present silently.

Lord, it can be truly said that You cradle Your children asleep in Your arms during this long night of faith, and that You are pleased to allow an infinite variety of thoughts to pass through their minds—thoughts that are holy and full of mystery. In the state in which these dreams of the night place them, they do indeed experience terrible torments of fear, anguish, and weariness, but on the bright day of glory, You will make them disappear and turn into joy.[13]

REV. JEAN-PIERRE DE CAUSSADE, S.J.

THE PRAYERS

Into your hands, O Lord, we commend our
   spirits; * For you have redeemed us, O Lord,
   O God of truth.
Keep us, O Lord, as the apple of your eye; *
   Hide us under the shadow of your wings.†

Lord, have mercy.
   Christ, have mercy.
Lord, have mercy.

Our Father in heaven,
   hallowed be your Name,
   your kingdom come,
   your will be done,
   on earth as in heaven.
Give us today our daily bread.
Forgive us our sins
   as we forgive those
   who sin against us.
Save us from the time of trial,
   and deliver us from evil.

For the kingdom, the power,
   and the glory are yours,
   now and for ever. Amen.

Lord, hear our prayer;
   And let our cry come to you.
Let us pray.

Keep watch, dear Lord, with those who work, or
watch, or weep this night, and give your angels
charge over those who sleep. Tend the sick, Lord
Christ; give rest to the weary, bless the dying,
soothe the suffering, pity the afflicted, shield the
joyous; and all for your love's sake. Amen.

Free intercessions and/or reflections may be offered.

THE REFLECTION

What do your nights teach you?
What are your dreams teaching you?

THE CONCLUSION

Lord, you now have set your servant free * to go
   in peace as you have promised;
For these eyes of mine have seen the Savior, *
   whom you have prepared for all the world to see:
A Light to enlighten the nations, * and the glory of
   your people Israel.

Glory to the Father, and to the Son, and to the
Holy Spirit: * as it was in the beginning, is now,
and will be for ever. Amen.

Guide us waking, O Lord, and guard us sleeping;
that awake we may watch with Christ, and asleep
we may rest in peace.

Let us bless the Lord.
Thanks be to God.

The almighty and merciful Lord, Father, Son, and
Holy Spirit, bless us and keep us. Amen.

THOUGHTS & MEMORIES

THURSDAY

THURSDAY MORNING PRAYER

THE INVITATION TO WORSHIP

Out of the deep have I called unto thee, O Lord: *
Lord, hear my voice.
The Lord is full of compassion and mercy: *
Come, let us adore him.
Glory to the Father, and to the Son, and to the
Holy Spirit: * as it was in the beginning, is
now, and will be for ever. Amen.

PSALM 35

Fight those who fight me, O LORD; * attack those
who are attacking me.
Take up shield and armor * and rise up to help me.
Draw the sword and bar the way against those
who pursue me; * say to my soul, "I am your
salvation."
Let those who seek after my life be shamed and
humbled; * let those who plot my ruin fall back
and be dismayed.
Let them be like chaff before the wind, * and let
the angel of the LORD drive them away.
Let their way be dark and slippery, * and let the
angel of the LORD pursue them.

For they have secretly spread a net for me without
a cause; * without a cause they have dug a pit
to take me alive.

Let ruin come upon them unawares; * let them be
caught in the net they hid; let them fall into the
pit they dug.

Then I will be joyful in the LORD; * I will glory in
his victory.

My very bones will say, "LORD, who is like you?
* You deliver the poor from those who are too
strong for them, the poor and needy from those
who rob them."

Malicious witnesses rise up against me; * they
charge me with matters I know nothing about.

They pay me evil in exchange for good; * my soul
is full of despair.

But when they were sick I dressed in sack-cloth *
and humbled myself by fasting;

I prayed with my whole heart, as one would for
a friend or a brother; * I behaved like one who
mourns for his mother, bowed down and grieving.

But when I stumbled, they were glad and gathered
together; they gathered against me; * strangers
whom I did not know tore me to pieces and
would not stop.

They put me to the test and mocked me; * they
gnashed at me with their teeth.

O LORD, how long will you look on? * rescue me
from the roaring beasts, and my life from the
young lions.

I will give you thanks in the great congregation; * I
will praise you in the mighty throng.

Do not let my treacherous foes rejoice over me, *
nor let those who hate me without a cause wink
at each other.

For they do not plan for peace, * but invent
deceitful schemes against the quiet in the land.

They opened their mouths at me and said, * "Aha!
we saw it with our own eyes."

You saw it, O LORD; do not be silent; * O Lord,
be not far from me.

Awake, arise, to my cause! * to my defense, my
God and my Lord!

Give me justice, O LORD my God, according to
your righteousness; * do not let them triumph
over me.

Do not let them say in their hearts, "Aha! just what
we want!" * Do not let them say, "We have
swallowed him up."

Let all who rejoice at my ruin be ashamed and
disgraced; * let those who boast against me be
clothed with dismay and shame.

Let those who favor my cause sing out with joy and
be glad; * let them say always, "Great is the LORD,
who desires the prosperity of his servant."

And my tongue shall be talking of your righteousness * and of your praise all the day long.

Glory to the Father, and to the Son, and to the
Holy Spirit: * as it was in the beginning, is now,
and will be for ever. Amen.

THE WORD

Jesus then went into the Temple and drove out all
those who were selling and buying there; he upset
the tables of the money-changers and the seats of
the dove-sellers. He said to them, "According to
scripture, *my house shall be called a house of prayer;* but
you are turning it into a bandits' den."

MATTHEW 21:12–13 (NJB)

Thanks be to God.

CANTICLE

THE SECOND SONG OF ISAIAH, ISAIAH 55:6–11

Seek the LORD while he wills to be found; * call
upon him when he draws near.

Let the wicked forsake their ways * and the evil
ones their thoughts;

And let them turn to the LORD, and he will have
compassion, * and to our God, for he will richly
pardon.

For my thoughts are not your thoughts, * nor your
ways my ways, says the LORD.

For as the heavens are higher than the earth, * so
    are my ways higher than your ways, and my
    thoughts than your thoughts.
For as rain and snow fall from the heavens * and
    return not again, but water the earth,
Bringing forth life and giving growth, * seed for
    sowing and bread for eating,
So is my word that goes forth from my mouth; * it
    will not return to me empty;
But it will accomplish that which I have purposed, *
    and prosper in that for which I sent it.
Glory to the Father, and to the Son, and to the
    Holy Spirit: * as it was in the beginning, is now,
    and will be for ever. Amen.

THE APOSTLES' CREED

I believe in God, the Father almighty, creator of
    heaven and earth.
I believe in Jesus Christ, his only Son, our Lord.
    He was conceived by the power of the
    Holy Spirit and born of the Virgin Mary.
    He suffered under Pontius Pilate, was
    crucified, died, and was buried.
    He descended to the dead.
    On the third day he rose again.
    He ascended into heaven, and is seated at
    the right hand of the Father.

He will come again to judge the living and
the dead.
I believe in the Holy Spirit, the holy catholic
Church, the communion of saints, the
forgiveness of sins, the resurrection of the
body, and the life everlasting. Amen.

THE PRAYERS

Our Father in heaven,
hallowed be your Name,
your kingdom come,
your will be done,
on earth as in heaven.
Give us today our daily bread.
Forgive us our sins
as we forgive those
who sin against us.
Save us from the time of trial,
and deliver us from evil.
For the kingdom, the power,
and the glory are yours,
now and for ever. Amen.

THE PETITIONS

Save your people, Lord, and bless your inheritance;
* Govern and uphold them, now and always.

Day by day we bless you; * We praise your Name
for ever.

Lord, keep us from all sin today; * Have mercy on
us; Lord, have mercy.

Lord, show us your love and mercy; * For we put
our trust in you.

In you, Lord, is our hope; * And we shall never
hope in vain.

For our *brother/sister N.*, let us pray to our Lord Jesus
Christ who said, "I am Resurrection, and I am
Life."

Lord, you consoled Martha and Mary in their
distress; draw near to us who mourn for *N.*, and
dry the tears of those who weep.

Hear us, Lord.

You wept at the grave of Lazarus, your friend;
comfort us in our sorrow.

Hear us, Lord.

You raised the dead to life; give to our *brother/sister*
eternal life.

Hear us, Lord.

You promised paradise to the thief who repented;
bring our *sister/brother* to the joys of heaven.

Hear us, Lord.

Our *brother/sister* was washed in Baptism and anointed with the Holy Spirit; give *him/her* fellowship with all your saints.

Hear us, Lord.

S/he was nourished with your Body and Blood; grant *her/him* a place at the table in your heavenly kingdom.

Hear us, Lord.

Comfort us in our sorrows at the death of *N.*; let our faith be our consolation, and eternal life our hope.†

Silence may follow.

THE COLLECT

Grant, O Lord, to all who are bereaved the spirit of faith and courage, that *we* may have strength to meet the day to come with steadfastness and patience; not sorrowing without hope, but in remembrance of your great goodness, and in the expectation of eternal life with those *we* love. And this *we* ask in the Name of Jesus Christ our Savior. Amen.†

THE MEDITATION

This may be read aloud by one person and followed by silence, or read by all present silently.

Meanwhile, where is God? This is one of the most disquieting symptoms. When you are happy, so happy that you have no sense of needing Him, so happy that you are tempted to feel His claims upon you as an interruption, if you remember yourself and turn to Him with gratitude and praise, you will be—or so it feels—welcomed with open arms. But go to Him when your need is desperate, when all other help is in vain, and what do you find? A door slammed in your face, and a sound of bolting and double bolting on the inside. After that, silence. You may as well turn away. The longer you wait, the more emphatic the silence will become. There are no lights in the windows. It might as well be an empty house. Was it ever inhabited? It seemed so once. And that seeming was as strong as this. What can this mean? Why is He so present a commander in our time of prosperity and so very absent a help in time of trouble?[14]

C.S. LEWIS

Free intercessions and/or reflections may be offered.

THE REFLECTION

You need look no further than the psalms to see that the Bible is full of angry people beloved by God. As this morning's readings demonstrate, Jesus felt angry and abandoned sometimes. Meditate on your anger—toward God, toward the living, toward the dead. And remember that God will not cast you out for feeling angry. In fact, bringing your anger to God may bring you closer to God.

THE CONCLUSION

Let us bless the Lord.
   Thanks be to God.

Keep alert, stand firm in your faith, be courageous, be strong. Let all that you do be done in love. Amen.

1 CORINTHIANS 16:13–14 (NRSV)

THURSDAY NOONDAY PRAYER

THE INVITATION TO WORSHIP

Take courage, my children, cry to God. * And he
   will deliver you from the power and hand of
   the enemy.

Glory to the Father, and to the Son, and to the
Holy Spirit: * as it was in the beginning, is
now, and will be for ever. Amen.

PSALM 57:1–3

Be merciful to me, O God, be merciful, for I have
taken refuge in you; * in the shadow of your
wings will I take refuge until this time of trouble
has gone by.
I will call upon the Most High God, * the God
who maintains my cause.
He will send from heaven and save me; * he will
confound those who trample upon me; God
will send forth his love and his faithfulness.
Glory to the Father, and to the Son, and to the
Holy Spirit: * as it was in the beginning, is now,
and will be for ever. Amen.

THE WORD

My soul is bereft of peace;
I have forgotten what happiness is;

So I say, "Gone is my glory,
and all that I had hoped for
from the LORD."

The thought of my affliction and my
homelessness,

is wormwood and gall!
My soul continually thinks of it
and is bowed down within me.

But this I call to mind,
and therefore I have hope:

The steadfast love of the LORD never ceases,
his mercies never come to an end;
they are new every morning;
great is your faithfulness.

"The LORD is my portion," says my soul,
"therefore I will hope in him."
The LORD is good to those who wait for him,
to the soul that seeks him.

For the LORD will not reject forever.
Although he causes grief,
he will have compassion,
according to the abundance of his steadfast love;
for he does not willingly afflict
or grieve anyone.

LAMENTATIONS 3:17–25, 31–33 (NRSV)

Thanks be to God.

THE MEDITATION

*This may be read aloud by one person and followed
by silence, or read by all present silently.*

God does not cheapen himself or us by offering easy answers to the anguished *Why?* that we who are human cannot help but ask. The mystery of life and death and suffering remains a mystery in all human generations, and it is no less a mystery for us. We don't get a quick fix from our faith.[15]

EDMUND LEE BROWNING

THE PRAYERS

Lord, have mercy.
    Christ, have mercy.
Lord, have mercy.

Our Father in heaven,
    hallowed be your Name,
    your kingdom come,
    your will be done,
    on earth as in heaven.
Give us today our daily bread.
Forgive us our sins
    as we forgive those
    who sin against us.
Save us from the time of trial,
    and deliver us from evil.
For the kingdom, the power,
    and the glory are yours,
    now and for ever. Amen.

THE COLLECT

O God of grace and glory, *we* remember before you this day *our* brother (sister) N. *We* thank you for giving *her/him* to *us*, to know and to love as a companion on *our* earthly pilgrimage. In your boundless compassion, console *us* who mourn. Give *us* faith to see in death the gate of eternal life, so that in quiet confidence *we* may continue *our* course on earth, until, by your call, *we* are reunited with those who have gone before; through Jesus Christ our Lord. Amen.†

Free intercessions and/or reflections may be offered.

THE REFLECTION

The Scripture for today claims that God "does not willingly afflict or grieve anyone." Have you ever asked the anguished "Why does suffering exist in the world if God is both all-powerful and all-loving?

THE CONCLUSION

Let us bless the Lord.
  Thanks be to God.

Rest eternal grant to N., O Lord,
And let light perpetual shine upon *him/her*.

THURSDAY EVENING PRAYER

❦

THE INVITATION TO WORSHIP

I am the Resurrection and I am the Life, says the
Lord, * Whoever has faith in me shall have life,
even though he die.
For if we have life, we are alive in the Lord, * And
if we die, we die in the Lord.
So, then, whether we live or die, * We are the
Lord's possession.†

O GRACIOUS LIGHT

O gracious Light,
pure brightness of the everliving Father in heaven,
O Jesus Christ, holy and blessed!
Now as we come to the setting of the sun,
and our eyes behold the vesper light,
we sing your praises, O God: Father, Son, and
Holy Spirit.†

PSALM 23 (KJV)

The Lord is my shepherd; * I shall not want.
He maketh me to lie down in green pastures; * he
leadeth me beside the still waters.

He restoreth my soul; * he leadeth me in the paths
of righteousness for his Name's sake.

Yea, though I walk through the valley of the shadow
of death, I will fear no evil; * for thou art with me;
thy rod and thy staff, they comfort me.

Thou preparest a table before me in the presence
of mine enemies; * thou anointest my head with
oil; my cup runneth over.

Surely goodness and mercy shall follow me all the
days of my life, * and I will dwell in the house
of the Lord for ever.

Glory to the Father, and to the Son, and to the
Holy Spirit: * as it was in the beginning, is now,
and will be for ever. Amen.

THE WORD

I am the good shepherd: the good shepherd lays
down his life for the sheep. The hired man, since
he is not the shepherd and the sheep do not
belong to him, abandons the sheep as soon as
he sees a wolf coming, and runs away, and then
the wolf attacks and scatters the sheep; he runs
away because he is only a hired man and has no
concern for his sheep.

I am the good shepherd; I know my own and
my own know me, just as the Father knows me
and I know the Father; and I lay down my life for

my sheep. And there are other sheep I have that are not of this fold, and I must lead these too. They too will listen to my voice, and there will be only one flock, one shepherd.

JOHN 10:11–16 (NJB)

Thanks be to God.

CANTICLE
THE SONG OF MARY, LUKE 1:46–55

My soul proclaims the greatness of the Lord, my spirit rejoices in God my Savior; * for he has looked with favor on his lowly servant.

From this day all generations will call me blessed: * the Almighty has done great things for me, and holy is his Name.

He has mercy on those who fear him * in every generation.

He has shown the strength of his arm, * he has scattered the proud in their conceit.

He has cast down the mighty from their thrones, * and has lifted up the lowly.

He has filled the hungry with good things, * and the rich he has sent away empty.

He has come to the help of his servant Israel, * for he has remembered his promise of mercy,

The promise he made to our fathers, * to Abraham and his children for ever.

Glory to the Father, and to the Son, and to the
Holy Spirit: * as it was in the beginning, is now,
and will be for ever. Amen.

THE APOSTLES' CREED

I believe in God, the Father almighty, creator of
heaven and earth.
I believe in Jesus Christ, his only Son, our Lord.
He was conceived by the power of the
Holy Spirit and born of the Virgin Mary.
He suffered under Pontius Pilate, was
crucified, died, and was buried.
He descended to the dead.
On the third day he rose again.
He ascended into heaven, and is seated at
the right hand of the Father.
He will come again to judge the living and
the dead.
I believe in the Holy Spirit, the holy catholic
Church, the communion of saints, the
forgiveness of sins, the resurrection of the
body, and the life everlasting. Amen.

THE PRAYERS

Our Father in heaven,
hallowed be your Name,
your kingdom come,

your will be done,
   on earth as in heaven.
Give us today our daily bread.
Forgive us our sins
   as we forgive those
   who sin against us.
Save us from the time of trial,
   and deliver us from evil.
For the kingdom, the power,
   and the glory are yours,
   now and for ever. Amen.

THE PETITION

Show us your mercy, O Lord; *
   And grant us your salvation.
Clothe your ministers with righteousness; *
   Let your people sing with joy.
Give peace, O Lord, in all the world; *
   For only in you can we live in safety.
Lord, keep this nation under your care; *
   And guide us in the way of justice and truth.
Let your way be known upon earth; *
   Your saving health among all nations.
Let not the needy, O Lord, be forgotten; *
   Nor the hope of the poor be taken away.
Create in us clean hearts, O God; *
   And sustain us with your Holy Spirit.

THE COLLECT

God of all, *we* pray to you for *N.*, and for all those whom *we* love but see no longer. Grant to them your peace; let light perpetual shine upon them; and, in your loving wisdom and almighty power, work in them the good purpose of your perfect will, through Christ our Lord. Amen.†

THE MEDITATION

This may be read aloud by one person and followed by silence, or read by all present silently.

Death is nothing at all. I have only slipped away into the next room. I am I and you are you. Whatever we were to each other, that we still are. Call me by my old familiar name, speak to me in the easy way which you always used. Put no difference in your tone; wear no forced air of solemnity or sorrow. Laugh as we always laughed at the little jokes we enjoyed together. Let my name be ever the household word that it always was, let it be spoken without effect, without the trace of a shadow on it. Life means all that it ever meant. It is the same as it ever was; there is unbroken continuity. Why should I be out of mind because I am out of sight? I am waiting for you, for an interval, somewhere very near, just round the corner. All is well.[16]   HENRY SCOTT HOLLAND

Free intercessions and/or reflections may be offered.

THE REFLECTION

When my husband died, I wanted to die too. It helped to have a little boy with soft baby skin who needed me, only me, to nurse him. It helped when a priest told me, "You belong here like the stars and the trees." It helped when I thought of Jesus between us, holding our hands. Maybe it will help you to read the 23rd Psalm while visualizing your loved ones and yourself belonging in the same fold, the flock of Christ. Know that Christ links the rooms of the living and the dead.

THE CONCLUSION

Let us bless the Lord.
  Thanks be to God.

May the God of hope fill you with all joy and peace in believing . . . by the power of the Holy Spirit. Amen.

ROMANS 15:13 (NRSV)

THURSDAY COMPLINE

THE INVITATION TO WORSHIP

The Lord Almighty grant us a peaceful night and a perfect end. Amen.

Answer me when I call, O God, defender of my
cause; * you set me free when I am hard-pressed;
have mercy on me and hear my prayer.

Glory to the Father, and to the Son, and to the
Holy Spirit: * as it was in the beginning, is now,
and will be for ever. Amen.

PSALM 31:1–11, 14–16, 24

In you, O LORD, have I taken refuge; let me never be
put to shame; * deliver me in your righteousness.

Incline your ear to me; * make haste to deliver me.

Be my strong rock, a castle to keep me safe, for
you are my crag and my stronghold; * for the
sake of your Name, lead me and guide me.

Take me out of the net that they have secretly set
for me, * for you are my tower of strength.

Into your hands I commend my spirit, * for you
have redeemed me, O LORD, O God of truth.

I hate those who cling to worthless idols, * and I
put my trust in the LORD.

I will rejoice and be glad because of your mercy; * for
you have seen my affliction; you know my distress.

You have not shut me up in the power of the
enemy; * you have set my feet in an open place.

Have mercy on me, O LORD, for I am in trouble;
* my eye is consumed with sorrow, and also my
throat and my belly.

For my life is wasted with grief, and my years with
sighing; * my strength fails me because of affliction, and my bones are consumed.

I have become a reproach to all my enemies and
even to my neighbors, a dismay to those of my
acquaintance; * when they see me in the street
they avoid me.

But as for me, I have trusted in you, O LORD. * I
have said, "You are my God.

My times are in your hand; * rescue me from the
hand of my enemies, and from those who per-
secute me.

Make your face to shine upon your servant, * and
in your loving-kindness save me."

Be strong and let your heart take courage, * all you
who wait for the LORD.

Glory to the Father, and to the Son, and to the
Holy Spirit: * as it was in the beginning, is now,
and will be forever. Amen.

THE WORD

Now that very same day, two of them were on
their way to a village called Emmaus, seven miles
from Jerusalem, and they were talking together
about all that had happened.

And it happened that as they were talking
together and discussing it, Jesus himself came

up and walked by their side; but their eyes were
prevented from recognizing him.

LUKE 24:13–16 (NJB)

The Word of the Lord.

THE MEDITATION

*This may be read aloud by one person and followed
by silence, or read by all present silently.*

"Lead, Kindly Light"

Lead, kindly Light, amid the encircling gloom;
    Lead thou me on;
The night is dark, and I am far from home;
    Lead thou me on;
Keep thou my feet; I do not ask to see
The distant scene; one step enough for me.

I was not ever thus, nor prayed that thou
    Shouldst lead me on;
I loved to choose and see my path; but now
    Lead thou me on;
I loved the garish day, and, spite of fears,
Pride ruled my will: remember not past years.

So long thy prayer hath blest me, sure it still
    Will lead me on
O'er moor and fen, o'er crag and torrent, till
    The night is gone;

And with the morn those angel faces smile
Which I have loved long since, and lost awhile.[17]
JOHN HENRY CARDINAL NEWMAN

THE PRAYERS

Into your hands, O Lord, we commend our
    spirits; * For you have redeemed us, O Lord, O
    God of truth.
Keep us, O Lord, as the apple of your eye; *
    Hide us under the shadow of your wings.†

Lord, have mercy.
    Christ, have mercy.
Lord, have mercy.
Our Father in heaven,
    hallowed be your Name,
    your kingdom come,
    your will be done,
    on earth as in heaven.
Give us today our daily bread.
Forgive us our sins
    as we forgive those
    who sin against us.
Save us from the time of trial,
    and deliver us from evil.
For the kingdom, the power,
    and the glory are yours,
    now and for ever. Amen.

Lord, hear our prayer;
  And let our cry come to you.

Let us pray.

Keep watch, dear Lord, with those who work, or watch, or weep this night, and give your angels charge over those who sleep. Tend the sick, Lord Christ; give rest to the weary, bless the dying, soothe the suffering, pity the afflicted, shield the joyous; and all for your love's sake. Amen.

Free intercessions and/or reflections may be offered.

THE REFLECTION

On the road to Emmaus, two of Jesus' followers didn't recognize their risen Lord. What keeps your eyes from recognizing God in your life? Can you remember times in the past when you felt God a kindly light leading you? To remember those times may make it easier for you, as the psalmist says, to put this time in God's hand and to know Christ's presence.

THE CONCLUSION

Lord, you now have set your servant free * to go
  in peace as you have promised;
For these eyes of mine have seen the Savior, *
  whom you have prepared for all the world to see:
A Light to enlighten the nations, * and the glory of
  your people Israel.

Glory to the Father, and to the Son, and to the
Holy Spirit: * as it was in the beginning, is now,
and will be for ever. Amen.

Guide us waking, O Lord, and guard us sleeping;
that awake we may watch with Christ, and asleep
we may rest in peace.

Let us bless the Lord.
   Thanks be to God.

The almighty and merciful Lord, Father, Son, and
Holy Spirit, bless us and keep us. Amen.

THOUGHTS & MEMORIES

FRIDAY

FRIDAY MORNING PRAYER

THE INVITATION TO WORSHIP

Out of the deep have I called unto thee, O Lord: *
Lord, hear my voice.

The Lord is full of compassion and mercy: *
Come, let us adore him.

Glory to the Father, and to the Son, and to the
Holy Spirit: * as it was in the beginning, is now,
and will be for ever. Amen.

PSALM 22:1–11

My God, my God, why have you forsaken me? *
and are so far from my cry and from the words
of my distress?

O my God, I cry in the daytime, but you do not
answer; * by night as well, but I find no rest.

Yet you are the Holy One, * enthroned upon the
praises of Israel.

Our forefathers put their trust in you; * they
trusted, and you delivered them.

They cried out to you and were delivered; * they
trusted in you and were not put to shame.

But as for me, I am a worm and no man, * scorned
  by all and despised by the people.
All who see me laugh me to scorn; * they curl their
  lips and wag their heads, saying,
"He trusted in the LORD; let him deliver him; * let
  him rescue him, if he delights in him."
Yet you are he who took me out of the womb, *
  and kept me safe upon my mother's breast.
I have been entrusted to you ever since I was born;
  * you were my God when I was still in my
  mother's womb.
Be not far from me, for trouble is near, * and there
  is none to help.
Glory to the Father, and to the Son, and to the
  Holy Spirit: * as it was in the beginning, is now,
  and will be for ever. Amen.

THE WORD

"My God, my God, why hast thou forsaken me?"
                 CHRIST ON THE CROSS, MATTHEW 27:46 (KJV)

The Word of the Lord.

CANTICLE

You are God: we praise you; * You are the Lord:
  we acclaim you; You are the eternal Father:

All creation worships you; * To you all angels, all
the powers of heaven, Cherubim and Seraphim,
sing in endless praise:

Holy, holy, holy Lord, God of power and might, *
heaven and earth are full of your glory.

The glorious company of apostles praise you. *
The noble fellowship of prophets praise you.
The white-robed army of martyrs praise you.

Throughout the world the holy Church acclaims
you; * Father, of majesty unbounded, your true
and only Son, worthy of all worship, and the
Holy Spirit, advocate and guide.

You, Christ, are the king of glory, * the eternal
Son of the Father.

When you became man to set us free * you did not
shun the Virgin's womb.

You overcame the sting of death * and opened the
kingdom of heaven to all believers.

You are seated at God's right hand in glory. * We
believe that you will come and be our judge.

Come then, Lord, and help your people, bought
with the price of your own blood, * and bring us
with your saints to glory everlasting.

Glory to the Father, and to the Son, and to the
Holy Spirit: * as it was in the beginning, is now,
and will be for ever. Amen.

THE APOSTLES' CREED

I believe in God, the Father almighty, creator of
heaven and earth.

I believe in Jesus Christ, his only Son, our Lord.
He was conceived by the power of the
Holy Spirit and born of the Virgin Mary.
He suffered under Pontius Pilate, was
crucified, died, and was buried.
He descended to the dead.
On the third day he rose again.
He ascended into heaven, and is seated at
the right hand of the Father.
He will come again to judge the living and
the dead.

I believe in the Holy Spirit, the holy catholic
Church, the communion of saints, the
forgiveness of sins, the resurrection of the
body, and the life everlasting. Amen.

THE PRAYERS

Our Father in heaven,
hallowed be your Name,
your kingdom come,
your will be done,
on earth as in heaven.
Give us today our daily bread.
Forgive us our sins

as we forgive those
who sin against us.
Save us from the time of trial,
and deliver us from evil.
For the kingdom, the power,
and the glory are yours,
now and for ever. Amen.

THE PETITIONS

Show us your mercy, O Lord; *
And grant us your salvation.
Clothe your ministers with righteousness; *
Let your people sing with joy.
Give peace, O Lord, in all the world; *
For only in you can we live in safety.
Lord, keep this nation under your care; *
And guide us in the way of justice and truth.
Let your way be known upon earth; *
Your saving health among all nations.
Let not the needy, O Lord, be forgotten; *
Nor the hope of the poor be taken away.
Create in us clean hearts, O God; *
And sustain us with your Holy Spirit.

For our *brother/sister* N., let us pray to our Lord
Jesus Christ who said, "I am Resurrection, and
I am Life."

Lord, you consoled Martha and Mary in their distress; draw near to us who mourn for *N.*, and dry the tears of those who weep.

Hear us, Lord.

You wept at the grave of Lazarus, your friend; comfort us in our sorrow.

Hear us, Lord.

You raised the dead to life; give to our *brother/sister* eternal life.

Hear us, Lord.

You promised paradise to the thief who repented; bring our *sister/brother* to the joys of heaven.

Hear us, Lord.

Our *brother/sister* was washed in Baptism and anointed with the Holy Spirit; give *him/her* fellowship with all your saints.

Hear us, Lord.

S/he was nourished with your Body and Blood; grant *her/him* a place at the table in your heavenly kingdom.

Hear us, Lord.

Comfort us in our sorrows at the death of *N.*; let our faith be our consolation, and eternal life our hope.†

Silence may follow.

THE COLLECT

Grant, O Lord, to all who are bereaved the spirit of faith and courage, that *we* may have strength to meet the day to come with steadfastness and patience; not sorrowing without hope, but in remembrance of your great goodness, and in the expectation of eternal life with those *we* love. And this *we* ask in the Name of Jesus Christ our Savior. Amen.†

THE MEDITATION

This may be read aloud by one person and followed by silence, or read by all present silently.

From "For the Fallen"

They shall not grow old, as we that are left to grow old:
Age shall not weary them, nor the years condemn.
At the going down of the sun and in the morning,
We will remember them.[18]   LAURENCE BINYON

Free intercessions and/or reflections may be offered.

THE REFLECTION

What kinds of feelings do Jesus' words "Why hast thou forsaken me?" bring up for you? Do you feel closer to Jesus,

*because you understand how he felt? Do you feel angry
with God for forsaking Jesus, or for forsaking anyone else?
Is remembering sometimes painful because of feeling forsaken?*

THE CONCLUSION

Let us bless the Lord.
Thanks be to God.

Keep alert, stand firm in your faith, be courageous,
be strong. Let all that you do be done in love.
Amen.

1 CORINTHIANS 16:13–14 (NRSV)

FRIDAY NOONDAY
PRAYER

THE INVITATION TO WORSHIP

Take courage, my children, cry to God. * And he
    will deliver you from the power and hand of
    the enemy.
Glory to the Father, and to the Son, and to the
    Holy Spirit: * as it was in the beginning, is
    now, and will be for ever. Amen.

PSALM 22:11–18

Be not far from me, for trouble is near, * and there
   is none to help.
Many young bulls encircle me; * strong bulls of
   Bashan surround me.
They open wide their jaws at me, * like a ravening
   and a roaring lion. I am poured out like water;
all my bones are out of joint; * my heart within
   my breast is melting wax. My mouth is dried
   out like a pot-sherd;
my tongue sticks to the roof of my mouth; * and
   you have laid me in the dust of the grave.
Packs of dogs close me in, and gangs of evildoers
   circle around me; * they pierce my hands and
   my feet; I can count all my bones.
They stare and gloat over me; * they divide my
   garments among them; they cast lots for my
   clothing.
Be not far away, O Lord; * you are my strength;
   hasten to help me.
Glory to the Father, and to the Son, and to the
   Holy Spirit: * as it was in the beginning, is now,
   and will be for ever. Amen.

THE WORD

When the sixth hour [noon] came there was
darkness over the whole land until the ninth

hour. And at the ninth hour Jesus cried out in a loud voice, "Eloi, Eloi, lama sabachthani?" which means, *"My God, my God, why have you forsaken me?"* When some of those who stood by heard this, they said, "Listen, he is calling on Elijah." Someone ran and soaked a sponge in vinegar and, putting it on a reed, gave it to him to drink saying, "Wait! And see if Elijah will come to take him down." But Jesus gave a loud cry and breathed his last. And the veil of the Sanctuary was torn in two from top to bottom. The centurion, who was standing in front of him, had seen how he had died, and he said, "In truth this man was Son of God."

MARK 15:33–39 (NJB)

The Word of the Lord.

THE MEDITATION

This may be read aloud by one person and followed by silence, or read by all present silently.

And I found comfort in weeping in your sight for her and for myself, in her behalf and my own. And I gave way to the tears I had been holding back, refreshing my heart with them, and it found rest in them, for it was in your ears, not in those of men who would have interpreted my weeping scornfully.[19]

AUGUSTINE OF HIPPO,
TO GOD ON THE DEATH OF HIS MOTHER

THE PRAYERS

Lord, have mercy.
  Christ, have mercy.
Lord, have mercy.
Our Father in heaven,
  hallowed be your Name,
  your kingdom come,
  your will be done,
  on earth as in heaven.
Give us today our daily bread.
Forgive us our sins
  as we forgive those
  who sin against us.
Save us from the time of trial,
  and deliver us from evil.
For the kingdom, the power,
  and the glory are yours,
  now and for ever. Amen.

THE COLLECT

O God of grace and glory, *we* remember before
you this day *our* brother (sister) N. *We* thank
you for giving *her/him* to *us*, to know and to
love as a companion on *our* earthly pilgrimage.
In your boundless compassion, console *us* who
mourn. Give *us* faith to see in death the gate of

eternal life, so that in quiet confidence *we* may continue *our* course on earth, until, by your call, *we* are reunited with those who have gone before; through Jesus Christ our Lord. Amen.†

Free intercessions and/or reflections may be offered.

THE REFLECTION

What is it that you are crying out to God? Is your crying out to God's ears different from your crying out to human ears?

THE CONCLUSION

Let us bless the Lord.
  Thanks be to God.

Rest eternal grant to *N.*, O Lord,
And let light perpetual shine upon *him/her.*

FRIDAY EVENING PRAYER

THE INVITATION TO WORSHIP

I am the Resurrection and I am the Life, says the Lord, * Whoever has faith in me shall have life, even though he die.

For if we have life, we are alive in the Lord, * And
  if we die, we die in the Lord.
So, then, whether we live or die, * We are the
  Lord's possession.†

O GRACIOUS LIGHT

O gracious Light,
pure brightness of the everliving Father in heaven,
O Jesus Christ, holy and blessed!
Now as we come to the setting of the sun,
and our eyes behold the vesper light,
we sing your praises, O God: Father, Son, and
Holy Spirit.†

PSALM 22:18–27

Be not far away, O LORD; * you are my strength;
  hasten to help me.
Save me from the sword, * my life from the power
  of the dog.
Save me from the lion's mouth, * my wretched
  body from the horns of wild bulls.
I will declare your Name to my brethren; * in the
  midst of the congregation I will praise you.
Praise the LORD, you that fear him; * stand in awe
  of him, O offspring of Israel; all you of Jacob's
  line, give glory.

For he does not despise nor abhor the poor in
their poverty; neither does he hide his face from
them; * but when they cry to him he hears them.

My praise is of him in the great assembly; * I will
perform my vows in the presence of those who
worship him.

The poor shall eat and be satisfied, and those who
seek the LORD shall praise him: * "May your
heart live for ever!"

All the ends of the earth shall remember and turn
to the LORD, * and all the families of the nations
shall bow before him.

For kingship belongs to the LORD; * he rules over
the nations.

Glory to the Father, and to the Son, and to the
Holy Spirit: * as it was in the beginning, is now,
and will be for ever. Amen.

THE WORD

On the evening of that first day of the week,
when the disciples were together, with the doors
locked for fear of the Jews, Jesus came and stood
among them and said, "Peace be with you!" After
he said this, he showed them his hands and side.
The disciples were overjoyed when they saw the
Lord. Again Jesus said, "Peace be with you! As the
Father has sent me, I am sending you." And with

that he breathed on them and said, "Receive the Holy Spirit."   JOHN 20:19–22 (NIV)

The Word of the Lord.

CANTICLE
THE SONG OF MARY, LUKE 1:46–55

My soul proclaims the greatness of the Lord, my
    spirit rejoices in God my Savior; * for he has
    looked with favor on his lowly servant.

From this day all generations will call me blessed:
    * the Almighty has done great things for me,
    and holy is his Name.

He has mercy on those who fear him * in every
    generation.

He has shown the strength of his arm, * he has
    scattered the proud in their conceit.

He has cast down the mighty from their thrones,
    * and has lifted up the lowly.

He has filled the hungry with good things, * and
    the rich he has sent away empty.

He has come to the help of his servant Israel, * for
    he has remembered his promise of mercy,

The promise he made to our fathers, * to Abraham
    and his children for ever.

Glory to the Father, and to the Son, and to the
    Holy Spirit: * as it was in the beginning, is now,
    and will be for ever. Amen.

THE APOSTLES' CREED

I believe in God, the Father almighty, creator of
heaven and earth.

I believe in Jesus Christ, his only Son, our Lord.
He was conceived by the power of the
Holy Spirit and born of the Virgin Mary.
He suffered under Pontius Pilate, was
crucified, died, and was buried.
He descended to the dead.
On the third day he rose again.
He ascended into heaven, and is seated at
the right hand of the Father.
He will come again to judge the living and
the dead.

I believe in the Holy Spirit, the holy catholic
Church, the communion of saints, the
forgiveness of sins, the resurrection of the
body, and the life everlasting. Amen.

THE PRAYERS

Our Father in heaven,
hallowed be your Name,
your kingdom come,
your will be done,
on earth as in heaven.
Give us today our daily bread.
Forgive us our sins

as we forgive those
who sin against us.
Save us from the time of trial,
and deliver us from evil.
For the kingdom, the power,
and the glory are yours,
now and for ever. Amen.

THE PETITION

Show us your mercy, O Lord; *
And grant us your salvation.
Clothe your ministers with righteousness; *
Let your people sing with joy.
Give peace, O Lord, in all the world; *
For only in you can we live in safety.
Lord, keep this nation under your care; *
And guide us in the way of justice and truth.
Let your way be known upon earth; *
Your saving health among all nations.
Let not the needy, O Lord, be forgotten; *
Nor the hope of the poor be taken away.
Create in us clean hearts, O God; *
And sustain us with your Holy Spirit.

THE COLLECT

God of all, *we* pray to you for *N.*, and for all those
whom *we* love but see no longer. Grant to them

your peace; let light perpetual shine upon them;
and, in your loving wisdom and almighty power,
work in them the good purpose of your perfect
will, through Jesus Christ our Lord. Amen.†

THE MEDITATION

*This may be read aloud by one person and followed
by silence, or read by all present silently.*

Jesus Christ is the same yesterday and today and
forever.   HEBREWS 13:8 (NIV)

Free intercessions and/or reflections may be offered.

THE REFLECTION

*What do you hear Jesus saying to you? In what ways does
Jesus appear to you? What about your loved one? Jesus
may be the same always, but in what ways are you different
in grief? In what ways are you unchanged?*

THE CONCLUSION

Let us bless the Lord.
  Thanks be to God.

May the God of hope fill you with all joy and
peace in believing . . . by the power of the Holy
Spirit. Amen.   ROMANS 15:13 (NRSV)

FRIDAY COMPLINE

THE INVITATION TO WORSHIP

The Lord Almighty grant us a peaceful night and a perfect end. Amen.

Answer me when I call, O God, defender of my cause; * you set me free when I am hard-pressed; have mercy on me and hear my prayer.

Glory to the Father, and to the Son, and to the Holy Spirit: * as it was in the beginning, is now, and will be for ever. Amen.

PSALM 22:26–30

All the ends of the earth shall remember and turn to the LORD, * and all the families of the nations shall bow before him.

For kingship belongs to the LORD; * he rules over the nations.

To him alone all who sleep in the earth bow down in worship; * all who go down to the dust fall before him.

My soul shall live for him; my descendants shall serve him; * they shall be known as the LORD's for ever.

They shall come and make known to a people yet unborn * the saving deeds that he has done.

Glory to the Father, and to the Son, and to the
Holy Spirit: * as it was in the beginning, is now,
and will be for ever. Amen.

THE WORD

Listen, I tell you a mystery: We will not all sleep,
but we will all be changed—in a flash, in the
twinkling of an eye. . . . For the perishable must
clothe itself with the imperishable, and the mortal
with immortality. When the perishable has been
clothed with the imperishable, and the mortal
with immortality, then the saying that is written
will come true:
"Death has been swallowed up in victory."
Where, O death, is your victory?
Where, O death, is your sting?"
But thanks be to God! He gives us the victory
through our Lord Jesus Christ.

1 CORINTHIANS 15:51–55, 57 (NIV)

Thanks be to God.

THE MEDITATION

*This may be read aloud by one person and followed
by silence, or read by all present silently.*

We hide death as if it were shameful and dirty.
We see in it only horror, meaninglessness, useless
struggle and suffering, and intolerable scandal—
whereas it is our life's culmination, its crowning
moment, and what gives it both sense and worth.[20]

MARIE DE HENNEZEL

THE PRAYERS

Into your hands, O Lord, we commend our
   spirits; * For you have redeemed us, O Lord,
   O God of truth.
Keep us, O Lord, as the apple of your eye; *
   Hide us under the shadow of your wings.†

Lord, have mercy.
   Christ, have mercy.
Lord, have mercy.

Our Father in heaven,
   hallowed be your Name,
   your kingdom come,
   your will be done,
   on earth as in heaven.
Give us today our daily bread.
Forgive us our sins
   as we forgive those
   who sin against us.
Save us from the time of trial,
   and deliver us from evil.

For the kingdom, the power,
   and the glory are yours,
   now and for ever. Amen.

Lord, hear our prayer;
   And let our cry come to you.
Let us pray.

Keep watch, dear Lord, with those who work, or
watch, or weep this night, and give your angels
charge over those who sleep. Tend the sick, Lord
Christ; give rest to the weary, bless the dying,
soothe the suffering, pity the afflicted, shield the
joyous; and all for your love's sake. Amen.

   Free intercessions and/or reflections may be offered.

THE REFLECTION

   *How do you think the death of Christ brings meaning to
   your life? Can you imagine what it is like for your loved one
   to be living in an immortal body?*

THE CONCLUSION

Lord, you now have set your servant free * to go
   in peace as you have promised;
For these eyes of mine have seen the Savior, *
   whom you have prepared for all the world to see:
A Light to enlighten the nations, * and the glory of
   your people Israel.

Glory to the Father, and to the Son, and to the
   Holy Spirit: * as it was in the beginning, is now,
   and will be for ever. Amen.

Guide us waking, O Lord, and guard us sleeping;
that awake we may watch with Christ, and asleep
we may rest in peace.

Let us bless the Lord.
   Thanks be to God.

The almighty and merciful Lord, Father, Son, and
Holy Spirit, bless us and keep us. Amen.

THOUGHTS & MEMORIES

SATURDAY

SATURDAY MORNING PRAYER

THE INVITATION TO WORSHIP

Out of the deep have I called unto thee, O Lord: *
Lord, hear my voice.

The Lord is full of compassion and mercy: *
Come, let us adore him.

Glory to the Father, and to the Son, and to the
Holy Spirit: * as it was in the beginning, is now,
and will be for ever. Amen.

PSALM 71:1–8

In you, O LORD, have I taken refuge; * let me
never be ashamed.

In your righteousness, deliver me and set me free;
* incline your ear to me and save me.

Be my strong rock, a castle to keep me safe; * you
are my crag and my stronghold.

Deliver me, my God, from the hand of the
wicked, * from the clutches of the evildoer and
the oppressor.

For you are my hope, O Lord GOD, * my
confidence since I was young.

I have been sustained by you ever since I was born; from my mother's womb you have been my strength; * my praise shall be always of you.

I have become a portent to many; * but you are my refuge and my strength.

Let my mouth be full of your praise * and your glory all the day long.

Glory to the Father, and to the Son, and to the Holy Spirit: * as it was in the beginning, is now, and will be for ever. Amen.

THE WORD

Therefore I tell you, do not worry about your life, what you will eat or drink; or about your body, what you will wear. Is not life more important than food, and the body more important than clothes?

Look at the birds of the air; they do not sow or reap or store away in barns, and yet your heavenly Father feeds them. Are you not much more valuable than they? Who of you by worrying can add a single hour to his life?

And why do you worry about clothes? See how the lilies of the field grow. They do not labor or spin. Yet I tell you that not even Solomon in all his splendor was dressed like one of these.

So do not worry, saying, "What shall we eat?" or "What shall we drink?" or "What shall we wear?" For your heavenly Father knows that you need them. But seek first his kingdom and his righteousness, and all these things will be given to you as well.   MATTHEW 6:25–29, 31, 32B–33 (NIV)

Thanks be to God.

CANTICLE
SONG OF THE REDEEMED, REVELATION 15:3–4

O ruler of the universe, Lord God, great deeds are they that you have done, * surpassing human understanding.

Your ways are ways of righteousness and truth, * O King of all the ages.

Who can fail to do you homage, Lord, and sing the praises of your Name? * for you only are the Holy One.

All nations will draw near and fall down before you, * because your just and holy works have been revealed.

Glory to the Father, and to the Son, and to the Holy Spirit: * as it was in the beginning, is now, and will be for ever. Amen.

THE APOSTLES' CREED

I believe in God, the Father almighty, creator of heaven and earth.

I believe in Jesus Christ, his only Son, our Lord.
   He was conceived by the power of the
   Holy Spirit and born of the Virgin Mary.
   He suffered under Pontius Pilate, was
   crucified, died, and was buried.
   He descended to the dead.
   On the third day he rose again.
   He ascended into heaven, and is seated at
   the right hand of the Father.
   He will come again to judge the living and
   the dead.
I believe in the Holy Spirit, the holy catholic
   Church, the communion of saints, the
   forgiveness of sins, the resurrection of the
   body, and the life everlasting. Amen.

THE PRAYERS

Our Father in heaven,
   hallowed be your Name,
   your kingdom come,
   your will be done,
   on earth as in heaven.
Give us today our daily bread.
Forgive us our sins
   as we forgive those
   who sin against us.
Save us from the time of trial,

and deliver us from evil.
For the kingdom, the power,
   and the glory are yours,
   now and for ever. Amen.

THE PETITIONS

Save your people, Lord, and bless your inheritance;
   * Govern and uphold them, now and always.
Day by day we bless you; * We praise your Name
   for ever.
Lord, keep us from all sin today; * Have mercy on
   us; Lord, have mercy.
Lord, show us your love and mercy; * For we put
   our trust in you.
In you, Lord, is our hope; * And we shall never
   hope in vain.

For our *brother/sister N.*, let us pray to our Lord Jesus
   Christ who said, "I am Resurrection, and I am
   Life."

Lord, you consoled Martha and Mary in their
   distress; draw near to us who mourn for *N.*, and
   dry the tears of those who weep.

Hear us, Lord.

You wept at the grave of Lazarus, your friend;
   comfort us in our sorrow.

Hear us, Lord.

You raised the dead to life; give to our *brother/sister* eternal life.

Hear us, Lord.

You promised paradise to the thief who repented; bring our *sister/brother* to the joys of heaven.

Hear us, Lord.

Our *brother/sister* was washed in Baptism and anointed with the Holy Spirit; give *him/her* fellowship with all your saints.

Hear us, Lord.

S/he was nourished with your Body and Blood; grant *her/him* a place at the table in your heavenly kingdom.

Hear us, Lord.

Comfort us in our sorrows at the death of *N.*; let our faith be our consolation, and eternal life our hope.†

Silence may follow.

THE COLLECT

Grant, O Lord, to all who are bereaved the spirit of faith and courage, that *we* may have strength to meet the day to come with steadfastness and patience; not sorrowing without hope, but in remembrance of your great goodness, and in the expectation of eternal life with those *we* love. And this *we* ask in the Name of Jesus Christ our Savior. Amen.†

THE MEDITATION

This may be read aloud by one person and followed by silence, or read by all present silently.

"On Anxiety About the Future"

The future is in God's hands, not yours. God will rule it, according to your need. But if you seek to forecast it in your own wisdom, you will gain nothing but anxiety and anticipation of inevitable trouble. Try only to make use of each day. Each day brings its own good and evil, and sometimes what seems evil becomes good if we leave it to God and do not forestall him with our impatience.[21]

FRANÇOIS FÉNELON

Free intercessions and/or reflections may be offered.

THE REFLECTION

Jesus points us toward the "lilies of the field" when we feel anxious. What are images that reduce your anxiety? What images help you "make use of each day"?

THE CONCLUSION

Let us bless the Lord.
Thanks be to God.

Keep alert, stand firm in your faith, be courageous, be strong. Let all that you do be done in
love. Amen.

1 CORINTHIANS 16:13–14 (NRSV)

SATURDAY NOONDAY
PRAYER

THE INVITATION TO WORSHIP

Take courage, my children, cry to God. * And he
will deliver you from the power and hand of
the enemy.
Glory to the Father, and to the Son, and to the
Holy Spirit: * as it was in the beginning, is now,
and will be for ever. Amen.

PSALM 90:1–6, 10, 12

Lord, you have been our refuge * from one generation to another.

Before the mountains were brought forth, or the
land and the earth were born, * from age to age
you are God.

You turn us back to the dust and say, * "Go back,
O child of earth."

For a thousand years in your sight are like yesterday
when it is past * and like a watch in the night.

You sweep us away like a dream; * we fade away
suddenly like the grass.

In the morning it is green and flourishes; * in the
evening it is dried up and withered.

The span of our life is seventy years, perhaps in
strength even eighty; * yet the sum of them
is but labor and sorrow, for they pass away
quickly and we are gone.

So teach us to number our days * that we may
apply our hearts to wisdom.

Glory to the Father, and to the Son, and to the
Holy Spirit: * as it was in the beginning, is now,
and will be for ever. Amen.

THE WORD

People were bringing little children to him, for
him to touch them. The disciples scolded them,
but when Jesus saw this he was indignant and
said to them, "Let the little children come to me;
do not stop them; for it is to such as these that

the kingdom of God belongs. In truth I tell you, anyone who does not welcome the kingdom of God like a little child will never enter it." Then he embraced them, laid his hands on them and gave them his blessing. MARK 10:13–16 (NJB)

Thanks be to God.

THE MEDITATION

This may be read aloud by one person and followed by silence, or read by all present silently.

Some of my richest experiences have come out of my most painful times . . . those that were the hardest to believe would ever turn into anything positive.[22] FRED ROGERS

THE PRAYERS

Lord, have mercy.
 Christ, have mercy.
Lord, have mercy.

Our Father in heaven,
 hallowed be your Name,
 your kingdom come,
 your will be done,
 on earth as in heaven.
Give us today our daily bread.
Forgive us our sins

as we forgive those
who sin against us.
Save us from the time of trial,
and deliver us from evil.
For the kingdom, the power,
and the glory are yours,
now and for ever. Amen.

THE COLLECT

O God of grace and glory, *we* remember before you this day *our* brother (sister) N. *We* thank you for giving *her/him* to *us*, to know and to love as a companion on *our* earthly pilgrimage. In your boundless compassion, console *us* who mourn. Give *us* faith to see in death the gate of eternal life, so that in quiet confidence *we* may continue *our* course on earth, until, by your call, *we* are reunited with those who have gone before; through Jesus Christ our Lord. Amen.†

Free intercessions and/or reflections may be offered.

THE REFLECTION

Some die so young, and others so old; some suffer with long disease, while others die unexpectedly. How is your grief making you more a child of God? What is your grief teaching you about what makes a life complete?

THE CONCLUSION

Let us bless the Lord.
 Thanks be to God.

Rest eternal grant to *N.*, O Lord,
And let light perpetual shine upon *him/her.*

SATURDAY EVENING PRAYER

THE INVITATION TO WORSHIP

I am the Resurrection and I am the Life, says the
    Lord, * Whoever has faith in me shall have life,
    even though he die.
For if we have life, we are alive in the Lord, * And
    if we die, we die in the Lord.
So, then, whether we live or die, * We are the
    Lord's possession.†

O GRACIOUS LIGHT

O gracious Light,
pure brightness of the everliving Father in heaven,
O Jesus Christ, holy and blessed!
Now as we come to the setting of the sun,

and our eyes behold the vesper light,
we sing your praises, O God: Father, Son, and
Holy Spirit.†

PSALM 130

Out of the depths have I called to you, O LORD;
 LORD, hear my voice; * let your ears consider
 well the voice of my supplication.

If you, LORD, were to note what is done amiss, * O
 Lord, who could stand?

For there is forgiveness with you; * therefore you
 shall be feared.

I wait for the LORD; my soul waits for him; * in his
 word is my hope.

My soul waits for the LORD, more than watchmen
 for the morning, * more than watchmen for the
 morning.

O Israel, wait for the LORD, * for with the LORD
 there is mercy;

With him there is plenteous redemption, * and he
 shall redeem Israel from all their sins.

Glory to the Father, and to the Son, and to the
 Holy Spirit: * as it was in the beginning, is now,
 and will be for ever. Amen.

THE WORD

On arriving, Jesus found that Lazarus had been in the tomb for four days already. Bethany is only about two miles from Jerusalem, and many Jews had come to Martha and Mary to comfort them about their brother. When Martha heard that Jesus was coming, she went to meet him. Mary remained sitting in the house. Martha said to Jesus, "Lord, if you had been here, my brother would not have died, but even now I know that God will grant you whatever you ask of him." Jesus said to her, "Your brother will rise again." Martha said to him, "I know he will rise again at the resurrection on the last day." Jesus said: "I am the resurrection. Anyone who believes in me, even though that person dies, will live, and whoever lives and believes in me will never die. Do you believe this?" "Yes, Lord," she said, "I believe that you are the Christ, the Son of God, the one who was to come into this world."

When she had said this, she went and called her sister Mary, saying in a low voice, "The Master is here and wants to see you." Hearing this, Mary got up quickly and went to him. Jesus had not yet come into the village; he was still at the place where Martha had met him. When the Jews who were in the house comforting Mary saw her get up so quickly and go out, they followed her, thinking that she was going to the tomb to weep there. Mary went to Jesus, and as soon as she saw him she threw herself at his feet, saying, "Lord, if you had been here, my brother would not have died." At the sight of her tears, and at those of the Jews who had come with her, Jesus was greatly distressed.   JOHN 11:17–33 (NJB)

The Word of the Lord.

CANTICLE

THE SONG OF MARY, LUKE 1:46–55

My soul proclaims the greatness of the Lord, my spirit rejoices in God my Savior; * for he has looked with favor on his lowly servant.

From this day all generations will call me blessed: * the Almighty has done great things for me, and holy is his Name.

He has mercy on those who fear him * in every generation.

He has shown the strength of his arm, * he has scattered the proud in their conceit.

He has cast down the mighty from their thrones, * and has lifted up the lowly.

He has filled the hungry with good things, * and the rich he has sent away empty.

He has come to the help of his servant Israel, * for
   he has remembered his promise of mercy,
The promise he made to our fathers, * to Abraham
   and his children for ever.
Glory to the Father, and to the Son, and to the
   Holy Spirit: * as it was in the beginning, is now,
   and will be for ever. Amen.

THE APOSTLES' CREED

I believe in God, the Father almighty, creator of
   heaven and earth.
I believe in Jesus Christ, his only Son, our Lord.
   He was conceived by the power of the
   Holy Spirit and born of the Virgin Mary.
   He suffered under Pontius Pilate, was
   crucified, died, and was buried.
   He descended to the dead.
   On the third day he rose again.
   He ascended into heaven, and is seated at
   the right hand of the Father.
   He will come again to judge the living and
   the dead.
I believe in the Holy Spirit, the holy catholic
   Church, the communion of saints, the
   forgiveness of sins, the resurrection of the
   body, and the life everlasting. Amen.

THE PRAYERS

Our Father in heaven,
hallowed be your Name,
your kingdom come,
your will be done,
on earth as in heaven.
Give us today our daily bread.
Forgive us our sins
as we forgive those
who sin against us.
Save us from the time of trial,
and deliver us from evil.
For the kingdom, the power,
and the glory are yours,
now and for ever. Amen.

THE PETITIONS

Show us your mercy, O Lord; *
And grant us your salvation.
Clothe your ministers with righteousness; *
Let your people sing with joy.
Give peace, O Lord, in all the world; *
For only in you can we live in safety.
Lord, keep this nation under your care; *
And guide us in the way of justice and truth.
Let your way be known upon earth; *

Your saving health among all nations.
Let not the needy, O Lord, be forgotten; *
    Nor the hope of the poor be taken away.
Create in us clean hearts, O God; *
    And sustain us with your Holy Spirit.

THE COLLECT

God of all, *we* pray to you for *N.*, and for all those
whom *we* love but see no longer. Grant to them
your peace; let light perpetual shine upon them;
and, in your loving wisdom and almighty power,
work in them the good purpose of your perfect
will, through Jesus Christ our Lord. Amen.†

THE MEDITATION

*This may be read aloud by one person and followed
by silence, or read by all present silently.*

You must observe that there are many kinds of
grief. . . . [Some] may even arise from charity,
which makes us pity our neighbors, as Our Lord
did when He raised Lazarus; and these do not
prevent union with the will of God. . . .[23]

TERESA OF AVILA

Free intercessions and/or reflections may be offered.

THE REFLECTION

For Teresa, the compassion of Christ leaps out of the story of Lazarus. What catches your attention? That Martha's grief is more active and more angry while Mary's is perhaps more paralyzing, and that yet Jesus responds to both of them? That Martha's grief brings her to a deeper knowledge of Jesus? The consoling friends? What would it have been like to have been one of those friends? To have been someone not mentioned, such as the mother of Martha, Mary, and Lazarus?

THE CONCLUSION

Let us bless the Lord.
  Thanks be to God.

May the God of hope fill you with all joy and peace in believing . . . by the power of the Holy Spirit. Amen.   ROMANS 15:13 (NRSV)

SATURDAY COMPLINE

THE INVITATION TO WORSHIP

The Lord Almighty grant us a peaceful night and a perfect end. Amen.

Answer me when I call, O God, defender of my
cause; * you set me free when I am hard-pressed;
have mercy on me and hear my prayer.

Glory to the Father, and to the Son, and to the
Holy Spirit: * as it was in the beginning, is now,
and will be for ever. Amen.

PSALM 77

I will cry aloud to God; * I will cry aloud, and he
will hear me.

In the day of my trouble I sought the Lord; * my
hands were stretched out by night and did not
tire; I refused to be comforted.

I think of God, I am restless, * I ponder, and my
spirit faints.

You will not let my eyelids close; * I am troubled
and I cannot speak.

I consider the days of old; * I remember the years
long past;

I commune with my heart in the night; * I ponder
and search my mind.

Will the Lord cast me off for ever? * will he no
more show his favor?

Has his loving-kindness come to an end for ever?
* has his promise failed for evermore?

Has God forgotten to be gracious? * has he, in his
anger, withheld his compassion?

And I said, "My grief is this: * the right hand of the
Most High has lost its power."

I will remember the works of the LORD, * and call
to mind your wonders of old time.

I will meditate on all your acts * and ponder your
mighty deeds.

Your way, O God, is holy; * who is so great a god
as our God?

You are the God who works wonders * and have
declared your power among the peoples.

By your strength you have redeemed your people,
* the children of Jacob and Joseph.

The waters saw you, O God; the waters saw you
and trembled; * the very depths were shaken.

The clouds poured out water; the skies thundered;
* your arrows flashed to and fro;

The sound of your thunder was in the whirlwind;
your lightnings lit up the world; * the earth
trembled and shook.

Your way was in the sea, and your paths in the great
waters, * yet your footsteps were not seen.

You led your people like a flock * by the hand of
Moses and Aaron.

Glory to the Father, and to the Son, and to the
Holy Spirit: * as it was in the beginning, is now,
and will be for ever. Amen.

THE WORD

In the beginning was the Word, and the Word
was with God, and the Word was God.

He was in the beginning with God. All things
came into being through him, and without him
not one thing came into being. What has come
into being in him was life, and the life was the
light of all people. The light shines in the darkness, and the darkness did not overcome it.

JOHN 1:1–5 (NRSV)

Thanks be to God.

THE MEDITATION

*This may be read aloud by one person and followed
by silence, or read by all present silently.*

O dying souls,
behold your living spring;
O dazzled eyes,
behold your sun of grace;
Dull ears, attend what
word this Word doth bring;
Up, heavy hearts,
with joy your joy embrace.
From death, from dark,
from deafness, from despairs,
This life, this light,

this Word,
this joy repairs.[24]

ROBERT SOUTHWELL—MODERNIZED

THE PRAYERS

Into your hands, O Lord, we commend our
    spirits; * For you have redeemed us, O Lord,
    O God of truth.
Keep us, O Lord, as the apple of your eye; *
    Hide us under the shadow of your wings.†

Lord, have mercy.
    Christ, have mercy.
Lord, have mercy.

Our Father in heaven,
    hallowed be your Name,
    your kingdom come,
    your will be done,
    on earth as in heaven.
Give us today our daily bread.
Forgive us our sins
    as we forgive those
    who sin against us.
Save us from the time of trial,
    and deliver us from evil.
For the kingdom, the power,
    and the glory are yours,
    now and for ever. Amen.

Keep watch, dear Lord, with those who work, or watch, or weep this night, and give your angels charge over those who sleep. Tend the sick, Lord Christ; give rest to the weary, bless the dying, soothe the suffering, pity the afflicted, shield the joyous; and all for your love's sake. Amen.

Free intercessions and/or reflections may be offered.

THE REFLECTION

What words of your loved one are you remembering tonight? Which of these words help you sleep? One way to think of Jesus as the Word is to think of Jesus as the one who breathed into your loved one the kindest, most loving, and life-giving words your loved one ever spoke to you.

THE CONCLUSION

Lord, you now have set your servant free * to go in peace as you have promised;

For these eyes of mine have seen the Savior, * whom you have prepared for all the world to see:

A Light to enlighten the nations, * and the glory of your people Israel.

Glory to the Father, and to the Son, and to the Holy Spirit: * as it was in the beginning, is now, and will be for ever. Amen.

Guide us waking, O Lord, and guard us sleeping;
that awake we may watch with Christ, and asleep
we may rest in peace.

Let us bless the Lord.
   Thanks be to God.

The almighty and merciful Lord, Father, Son, and
Holy Spirit, bless us and keep us. Amen.

THOUGHTS & MEMORIES

SUNDAY

SUNDAY MORNING PRAYER

THE INVITATION TO WORSHIP

Out of the deep have I called unto thee, O Lord: *
Lord, hear my voice.

The Lord is full of compassion and mercy: *
Come, let us adore him.

Glory to the Father, and to the Son, and to the
Holy Spirit: * as it was in the beginning, is now,
and will be for ever. Amen.

PSALM 62:1–9

For God alone my soul in silence waits; * from him
comes my salvation.

He alone is my rock and my salvation, * my
stronghold, so that I shall not be greatly shaken.

How long will you assail me to crush me, all of
you together, * as if you were a leaning fence,
a toppling wall?

They seek only to bring me down from my place
of honor; * lies are their chief delight.

They bless with their lips, * but in their hearts
they curse.

For God alone my soul in silence waits; * truly, my
hope is in him.

He alone is my rock and my salvation, * my
  stronghold, so that I shall not be shaken.
In God is my safety and my honor; * God is my
  strong rock and my refuge.
Put your trust in him always, O people, * pour out
  your hearts before him, for God is our refuge.
Glory to the Father, and to the Son, and to the
  Holy Spirit: * as it was in the beginning, is now,
  and will be for ever. Amen.

THE WORD

After the Sabbath, and towards dawn on the first
day of the week, Mary of Magdala and the other
Mary went to visit the sepulchre.

And suddenly there was a violent earthquake,
for an angel of the Lord, descending from heaven,
came and rolled away the stone and sat on it. His
face was like lightning, his robe white as snow.
The guards were so shaken by fear of him that
they were like dead men.

But the angel spoke; and he said to the women,
"There is no need for you to be afraid. I know you
are looking for Jesus, who was crucified. He is not
here, for he has risen, as he said he would. Come
and see the place where he lay, then go quickly
and tell his disciples, 'He has risen from the dead
and now he is going ahead of you to Galilee; that
is where you will see him.' Look! I have told you."

Filled with awe and great joy the women came quickly away from the tomb and ran to tell his disciples. And suddenly, coming to meet them, was Jesus. "Greetings," he said. And the women came up to him and, clasping his feet, they did him homage.   MATTHEW 28:1–9 (NJB)

Thanks be to God.

CANTICLE
THE SONG OF ZECHARIAH, LUKE 1:68–79

Blessed be the Lord, the God of Israel; * he has come to his people and set them free.

He has raised up for us a mighty savior, * born of the house of his servant David.

Through his holy prophets he promised of old that he would save us from our enemies, * from the hands of all who hate us.

He promised to show mercy to our fathers * and to remember his holy covenant.

This was the oath he swore to our father
Abraham, * to set us free from the hands of our enemies,

Free to worship him without fear, * holy and righteous in his sight all the days of our life.

You, my child, shall be called the prophet of the Most High, * for you will go before the Lord to prepare his way,

To give his people knowledge of salvation * by
the forgiveness of their sins.

In the tender compassion of our God * the dawn
from on high shall break upon us,

To shine on those who dwell in darkness and the
shadow of death, * and to guide our feet into
the way of peace.

Glory to the Father, and to the Son, and to the
Holy Spirit: * as it was in the beginning, is now,
and will be for ever. Amen.

THE APOSTLES' CREED

I believe in God, the Father almighty, creator of
heaven and earth.

I believe in Jesus Christ, his only Son, our Lord.
He was conceived by the power of the
Holy Spirit and born of the Virgin Mary.
He suffered under Pontius Pilate, was
crucified, died, and was buried.
He descended to the dead.
On the third day he rose again.
He ascended into heaven, and is seated at
the right hand of the Father.
He will come again to judge the living and
the dead.

I believe in the Holy Spirit, the holy catholic
Church, the communion of saints, the

forgiveness of sins, the resurrection of the
body, and the life everlasting. Amen.

THE PRAYERS

Our Father in heaven,
   hallowed be your Name,
   your kingdom come,
   your will be done,
   on earth as in heaven.
Give us today our daily bread.
Forgive us our sins
   as we forgive those
   who sin against us.
Save us from the time of trial,
   and deliver us from evil.
For the kingdom, the power,
   and the glory are yours,
   now and for ever. Amen.

THE PETITIONS

Show us your mercy, O Lord; *
   And grant us your salvation.
Clothe your ministers with righteousness; *
   Let your people sing with joy.
Give peace, O Lord, in all the world; *
   For only in you can we live in safety.

Lord, keep this nation under your care; *
  And guide us in the way of justice and truth.
Let your way be known upon earth; *
  Your saving health among all nations.
Let not the needy, O Lord, be forgotten; *
  Nor the hope of the poor be taken away.
Create in us clean hearts, O God; *
  And sustain us with your Holy Spirit.

For our *brother/sister N.*, let us pray to our Lord
  Jesus Christ who said, "I am Resurrection, and
  I am Life."

Lord, you consoled Martha and Mary in their
  distress; draw near to us who mourn for *N.*, and
  dry the tears of those who weep.

Hear us, Lord.

You wept at the grave of Lazarus, your friend;
  comfort us in our sorrow.

Hear us, Lord.

You raised the dead to life; give to our *brother/sister*
  eternal life.

Hear us, Lord.

You promised paradise to the thief who repented;
  bring our *sister/brother* to the joys of heaven.

Hear us, Lord.

Our *brother/sister* was washed in Baptism and anointed with the Holy Spirit; give *him/her* fellowship with all your saints.

Hear us, Lord.

S/he was nourished with your Body and Blood; grant *her/him* a place at the table in your heavenly kingdom.

Hear us, Lord.

Comfort us in our sorrows at the death of *N.*; let our faith be our consolation, and eternal life our hope.†

Silence may follow.

THE COLLECT

Grant, O Lord, to all who are bereaved the spirit of faith and courage, that *we* may have strength to meet the day to come with steadfastness and patience; not sorrowing without hope, but in remembrance of your great goodness, and in the expectation of eternal life with those *we* love. And this *we* ask in the Name of Jesus Christ our Savior. Amen.†

THE MEDITATION

This may be read aloud by one person and followed by silence, or read by all present silently.

"After Great Pain"

After great pain, a formal feeling comes—
The Nerves sit ceremonious, like Tombs—
The stiff Heart questions was it He, that bore,
And Yesterday, or Centuries before?
The Feet, mechanical, go round—
Of Ground, or Air, or Ought
A Wooden way
Regardless grown,
A Quartz contentment, like a stone—

This is the Hour of Lead—
Remembered, if outlived,
As Freezing persons recollect the Snow—
First Chill—then Stupor—then the letting go—[25]

EMILY DICKINSON

Free intercessions and/or reflections may be offered.

THE REFLECTION

*Are there any elements of waiting in your grief? For what do
you wait? How do you feel when you are waiting—silent,
like this morning's psalmist? Frozen—like Emily Dickinson?
What do you think the waiting was like for the Marys and
Jesus' other followers? How do you imagine the risen Christ?
Your risen loved one?*

THE CONCLUSION

Let us bless the Lord.
Thanks be to God.

Keep alert, stand firm in your faith, be courageous,
be strong. Let all that you do be done in love.
Amen.   1 CORINTHIANS 16:13–14 (NRSV)

SUNDAY NOONDAY PRAYER

THE INVITATION TO WORSHIP

Take courage, my children, cry to God. * And he
   will deliver you from the power and hand of
   the enemy.
Glory to the Father, and to the Son, and to the
   Holy Spirit: * as it was in the beginning, is now,
   and will be for ever. Amen.

PSALM 6:2–4, 6–9

Have pity on me, LORD, for I am weak; * heal me,
   LORD, for my bones are racked.
My spirit shakes with terror; * how long, O LORD,
   how long?

Turn, O LORD, and deliver me; * save me for your
   mercy's sake.
I grow weary because of my groaning; * every night
   I drench my bed and flood my couch with tears.
My eyes are wasted with grief * and worn away
   because of all my enemies.
Depart from me, all evildoers, * for the LORD has
   heard the sound of my weeping.
The LORD has heard my supplication; * the LORD
   accepts my prayer.
Glory to the Father, and to the Son, and to the
   Holy Spirit: * as it was in the beginning, is now,
   and will be for ever. Amen.

THE WORD

Thus says the LORD:
A voice is heard in Ramah,
lamentation and bitter weeping.
Rachel is weeping for her children;
she refuses to be comforted for her children,
because they are no more.

My joy is gone, grief is upon me,
my heart is sick.
Hark, the cry of my poor people
from far and wide in the land:
"Is the LORD not in Zion?
Is her King not in her? . . .

The harvest is past,
the summer is ended,
and we are not saved."
For the hurt of my poor people I am hurt,
I mourn, and dismay has taken hold of me.
Is there no balm in Gilead?
Is there no physician there?
Why then has the health of my poor people
not been restored?
O that my head were a spring of water,
and my eyes a fountain of tears,
so that I might weep day and night
for the slain of my poor people!

Blessed are those who trust in the LORD,
whose trust is the LORD.
They shall be like a tree planted by water,
sending out its roots by the stream.
It shall not fear when heat comes,
and its leaves shall stay green;
in the year of drought it is not anxious,
and it does not cease to bear fruit.

JEREMIAH 31:15, 8:18–9:1, 17:7–8 (NRSV)

The Word of the Lord.

THE MEDITATION

*This may be read aloud by one person and followed
by silence, or read by all present silently.*

How much there is to learn of love, that feeling of
the body and the soul, that teaches us what God
is, that He is love.[26]   DOROTHY DAY

THE PRAYERS

Lord, have mercy.
  Christ, have mercy.
Lord, have mercy.

Our Father in heaven,
  hallowed be your Name,
  your kingdom come,
  your will be done,
  on earth as in heaven.
Give us today our daily bread.
Forgive us our sins
  as we forgive those
  who sin against us.
Save us from the time of trial,
  and deliver us from evil.
For the kingdom, the power,
  and the glory are yours,
  now and for ever. Amen.

THE COLLECT

O God of grace and glory, *we* remember before
you this day *our* brother (sister) N. *We* thank

you for giving *her/him* to *us*, to know and to love as a companion on *our* earthly pilgrimage. In your boundless compassion, console *us* who mourn. Give *us* faith to see in death the gate of eternal life, so that in quiet confidence *we* may continue *our* course on earth, until, by your call, *we* are reunited with those who have gone before; through Jesus Christ our Lord. Amen.†

Free intercessions and/or reflections may be offered.

THE REFLECTION

In Jeremiah, the heartsick Lord longs for enough tears to cry without ceasing. Do you believe God is mourning with you? What are you learning about God's love, about God's being love, in your grief? Do you think grief is expanding your compassion?

THE CONCLUSION

Let us bless the Lord.
  Thanks be to God.

Rest eternal grant to *N.*, O Lord,
And let light perpetual shine upon *him/her*.

SUNDAY EVENING
PRAYER

THE INVITATION TO WORSHIP

I am the Resurrection and I am the Life, says the
Lord, * Whoever has faith in me shall have life,
even though he die.

For if we have life, we are alive in the Lord, * And
if we die, we die in the Lord.

So, then, whether we live or die, * We are the
Lord's possession.†

O GRACIOUS LIGHT

O gracious Light,
pure brightness of the everliving Father in heaven,
O Jesus Christ, holy and blessed!
Now as we come to the setting of the sun,
and our eyes behold the vesper light,
we sing your praises, O God: Father, Son, and
Holy Spirit.†

PSALM 126

When the LORD restored the fortunes of Zion, *
then were we like those who dream.

Then was our mouth filled with laughter, * and our tongue with shouts of joy.

Then they said among the nations, * "The LORD has done great things for them."

The LORD has done great things for us, * and we are glad indeed.

Restore our fortunes, O LORD, * like the water-courses of the Negev.

Those who sowed with tears * will reap with songs of joy.

Those who go out weeping, carrying the seed, * will come again with joy, shouldering their sheaves.

Glory to the Father, and to the Son, and to the Holy Spirit: * as it was in the beginning, is now, and will be for ever. Amen.

THE WORD

For all who are led by the Spirit of God are children of God. For you did not receive a spirit of slavery to fall back into fear, but you have received a spirit of adoption. When we cry, "Abba! Father!" it is that very Spirit bearing witness with our spirit that we are children of God, and if children, then heirs, heirs of God and joint heirs with Christ—if, in fact, we suffer with him so that we may also be glorified with him.

I consider that the sufferings of this present time are not worth comparing with the glory about to revealed to us. For the creation waits with eager longing for the revealing of the children of God.

ROMANS 8:14–19 (NRSV)

Thanks be to God.

CANTICLE
THE SONG OF MARY, LUKE 1:46–55

My soul proclaims the greatness of the Lord, my spirit rejoices in God my Savior; * for he has looked with favor on his lowly servant.

From this day all generations will call me blessed: * the Almighty has done great things for me, and holy is his Name.

He has mercy on those who fear him * in every generation.

He has shown the strength of his arm, * he has scattered the proud in their conceit.

He has cast down the mighty from their thrones, * and has lifted up the lowly.

He has filled the hungry with good things, * and the rich he has sent away empty.

He has come to the help of his servant Israel, * for he has remembered his promise of mercy,

The promise he made to our fathers, * to Abraham and his children for ever.

Glory to the Father, and to the Son, and to the Holy Spirit: * as it was in the beginning, is now, and will be for ever. Amen.

THE APOSTLES' CREED

I believe in God, the Father almighty, creator of heaven and earth.
I believe in Jesus Christ, his only Son, our Lord.
He was conceived by the power of the Holy Spirit and born of the Virgin Mary.
He suffered under Pontius Pilate, was crucified, died, and was buried.
He descended to the dead.
On the third day he rose again.
He ascended into heaven, and is seated at the right hand of the Father.
He will come again to judge the living and the dead.
I believe in the Holy Spirit, the holy catholic Church, the communion of saints, the forgiveness of sins, the resurrection of the body, and the life everlasting. Amen.

THE PRAYERS

Our Father in heaven,
hallowed be your Name,
your kingdom come,

your will be done,

on earth as in heaven.

Give us today our daily bread.

Forgive us our sins

as we forgive those

who sin against us.

Save us from the time of trial,

and deliver us from evil.

For the kingdom, the power,

and the glory are yours,

now and for ever. Amen.

THE PETITIONS

Show us your mercy, O Lord; *

And grant us your salvation.

Clothe your ministers with righteousness; *

Let your people sing with joy.

Give peace, O Lord, in all the world; *

For only in you can we live in safety.

Lord, keep this nation under your care; *

And guide us in the way of justice and truth.

Let your way be known upon earth; *

Your saving health among all nations.

Let not the needy, O Lord, be forgotten; *

Nor the hope of the poor be taken away.

Create in us clean hearts, O God; *

And sustain us with your Holy Spirit.

THE COLLECT

God of all, *we* pray to you for *N.*, and for all those whom *we* love but see no longer. Grant to them your peace; let light perpetual shine upon them; and, in your loving wisdom and almighty power, work in them the good purpose of your perfect will, through Jesus Christ our Lord. Amen.†

THE MEDITATION

This may be read aloud by one person and followed by silence, or read by all present silently.

Take courage, my children, call on God:
he will deliver you from tyranny,
from the clutches of your enemies;
for I look to the Eternal for your rescue,
and joy has come to me from the Holy One
at the mercy soon to reach you
from your Savior, the Eternal.
In sorrow and tears I watched you go away,
but God will give you back to me in joy and gladness for ever.

BARUCH 4:21–23 (NJB)

Free intercessions and/or reflections may be offered.

THE REFLECTION

What do you think Paul means by the "spirit of adoption"? What would you say to Paul, to this evening's psalmist, and to the author of the Book of Baruch about their belief that our sorrow and weeping will be transformed into eternal songs of joy and gladness? How could there be a relationship between the seeds of sorrow and the sheaves of joy?

THE CONCLUSION

Let us bless the Lord.
   Thanks be to God.

May the God of hope fill you with all joy and peace in believing . . . by the power of the Holy Spirit. Amen.

ROMANS 15:13 (NRSV)

SUNDAY COMPLINE

THE INVITATION TO WORSHIP

The Lord Almighty grant us a peaceful night and a perfect end. Amen.

Answer me when I call, O God, defender of my
cause; * you set me free when I am hard-pressed;
have mercy on me and hear my prayer.

Glory to the Father, and to the Son, and to the
Holy Spirit: * as it was in the beginning, is now,
and will be for ever. Amen.

PSALM 107:28–31

Then they cried to the LORD in their trouble, *
and he delivered them from their distress.

He stilled the storm to a whisper * and quieted the
waves of the sea.

Then were they glad because of the calm, * and he
brought them to the harbor they were bound
for.

Let them give thanks to the LORD for his mercy *
and the wonders he does for his children.

Glory to the Father, and to the Son, and to the
Holy Spirit: * as it was in the beginning, is now,
and will be for ever. Amen.

THE WORD

For thus said the Lord GOD, the Holy One of
Israel: In returning and rest you shall be saved; in
quietness and in trust shall be your strength.

ISAIAH 30:15 (NRSV)

Thanks be to God.

THE MEDITATION

*This may be read aloud by one person and followed
by silence, or read by all present silently.*

"Keeping Calm in Difficulty"

It is a great step forward, when in times of trouble,
distress, persecution and darkness, we can keep
still before God. With a calm and restful heart let
us wait in His presence, assured that He will give
us the victory. Let earth crumble; let our plans
fall to the ground; let all things give way around
us—our God is steadying the Ark, so let us wait,
trust and look to Him, and all will be well.[27]

HENRY FOSTER

THE PRAYERS

Into your hands, O Lord, we commend our
spirits; * For you have redeemed us, O Lord,
O God of truth.
Keep us, O Lord, as the apple of your eye; *
Hide us under the shadow of your wings.†

Lord, have mercy.
Christ, have mercy.
Lord, have mercy.

Our Father in heaven,
hallowed be your Name,
your kingdom come,

your will be done,
on earth as in heaven.
Give us today our daily bread.
Forgive us our sins
as we forgive those
who sin against us.
Save us from the time of trial,
and deliver us from evil.
For the kingdom, the power,
and the glory are yours,
now and for ever. Amen.

Lord, hear our prayer;
And let our cry come to you.
Let us pray.

Keep watch, dear Lord, with those who work, or watch, or weep this night, and give your angels charge over those who sleep. Tend the sick, Lord Christ; give rest to the weary, bless the dying, soothe the suffering, pity the afflicted, shield the joyous; and all for your love's sake. Amen.

Free intercessions and/or reflections may be offered.

THE REFLECTION

Henry Foster was a nineteenth-century physician who believed that spiritual healing is the most important component of health. Accordingly, he founded a sanitarium for ministers, missionaries, and teachers in Clifton Springs, New York. The foregoing meditation is taken from one of his chapel talks.

If you could create the perfect place to fix your mind on God, what would it be like? What kind of place can you create in your mind for returning and rest?

THE CONCLUSION

Lord, you now have set your servant free * to go
in peace as you have promised;
For these eyes of mine have seen the Savior, *
whom you have prepared for all the world to see:
A Light to enlighten the nations, * and the glory of
your people Israel.
Glory to the Father, and to the Son, and to the
Holy Spirit: * as it was in the beginning, is now,
and will be for ever. Amen.

Guide us waking, O Lord, and guard us sleeping;
that awake we may watch with Christ, and asleep
we may rest in peace.

Let us bless the Lord.
Thanks be to God.

The almighty and merciful Lord, Father, Son, and
Holy Spirit, bless us and keep us. Amen.

THOUGHTS & MEMORIES

CONFESSION OF SIN

If you feel that confessing sin is helpful to you, by all means include it in the Daily Offices. The Confession is traditionally said at Morning and Evening Prayer, and at Compline following the Invitation to Worship and prior to the Psalm. Below is the Confession of Sin as found in The Book of Common Prayer *on page 79 and elsewhere. (New York: Church Publishing, 1979)*

The Officiant says to the people

Dearly beloved, we have come together in the presence of Almighty God our heavenly Father, to set forth his praise, to hear his holy Word, and to ask, for ourselves and on behalf of others, those things that are necessary for our life and our salvation. And so that we may prepare ourselves in heart and mind to worship him, let us kneel in silence, and with penitent and obedient hearts confess our sins, that we may obtain forgiveness by his infinite goodness and mercy.

or this

Let us confess our sins against God and our neighbor.

Silence may be kept.

Officiant and People together, all kneeling

Most merciful God,
we confess that we have sinned against you
in thought, word, and deed,
by what we have done,
and by what we have left undone.
We have not loved you with our whole heart;
we have not loved our neighbors as ourselves.
We are truly sorry and we humbly repent.
For the sake of your Son Jesus Christ,
have mercy on us and forgive us;
that we may delight in your will,
and walk in your ways,
to the glory of your Name. Amen.

The Priest alone stands and says

Almighty God have mercy on you, forgive you
all your sins through our Lord Jesus Christ,
strengthen you in all goodness, and by the power
of the Holy Spirit keep you in eternal life. *Amen.*

*A deacon or lay person using the preceding form remains kneeling,
and substitutes "us" for "you" and "our" for "your."*

NOTES

1 *Praying the Hours*, Suzanne Guthrie. (Cambridge, MA: Cowley Publications, 2000), p. 3.

2 *The Divine Hours: Prayers for Summertime*, Compiled and Edited by Phyllis Tickle. (New York: Doubleday, 2000), p. ix.

3 *Morning and Evening Prayer with Selected Psalms and Readings for the Church Year*, Compiled and Edited by Howard Galley. (New York: Church Hymnal Corporation, 1994).

4 *The Book of Common Prayer*, The Episcopal Church (New York: Church Publishing, 1979), p. 504.

5 "Forever," John Boyle O'Reilly.

6 *The Little Prince*, Antoine de Saint-Exupery. Translated by Katherine Wood. (Orlando, FL: Harcourt, 1943/1982), p. 70.

7 *The Imitation of Christ*, Thomas à Kempis. (Brewster, MA: Paraclete Press, 1982), p. 201.

8 *The Wisdom of Julian of Norwich* (Grand Rapids, MI: Wm. B. Eerdmans Publishing Co., 1997), p. 64.

9 *Letters and Papers from Prison*, Dietrich Bonhoeffer. Edited by Eberhard Bethge. (New York: Collier Books, 1972), p. 176.

10 *Meditations on the Heart of God*, François Fénelon. (Brewster, MA: Paraclete Press, 1997), p. 29.

11 *The Temple: The Poetry of George Herbert*, edited by Henry Carrigan. (Brewster, MA: Paraclete Press, 2001), pp. 164–165.

12 *The Practice of the Presence of God*, Brother Lawrence. (Brewster, MA: Paraclete Press, 1985), p. 136.

13 *The Joy of Full Surrender*, Jean-Pierre de Caussade. (Brewster, MA: Paraclete Press, 1986), p. 168.

14 *A Grief Observed*, C.S. Lewis (New York: Bantam Books, 1976), pp. 4–5.

15 *A Year of Days with the Book of Common Prayer*, Edmund Lee Browning. (New York: Ballentine Wellspring, 1997), January 7 entry.

16 "Death Is Nothing at All," Henry Scott Holland (1847–1918), Canon of St. Paul's Cathedral, London.

17 *Lead, Kindly Light*, John Henry Cardinal Newman. (Brewster, MA: Paraclete Press, 1987), p. 1.

18 "For the Fallen," Laurence Binyon, in *The Oxford Book of War Poetry*, Edited by John Stallworthy. (Oxford: Oxford University Press, 1984), p. 209.

19 *The Confessions of St. Augustine*, Augustine of Hippo. (Brewster, MA: Paraclete Press, 1986), p. 175.

20 *Intimate Death: How the Dying Teach Us How to Live*, Marie de Hennezel, Translated by Carol Brown Janeway. (New York: Alfred Knopf, 1997), p. xi.

21 *The Royal Way of the Cross*, François Fénelon. (Brewster, MA: Paraclete Press, 1982), p. 27.

22 *You Are Special*, Fred Rogers. (New York: Penguin Books, 1994), p. 103.

23 *Interior Castle*, Teresa of Ávila, Translated and Edited by E. Allison Peers. (New York: Image Books, Doubleday, 1961/1989), p. 113.

24 "The Nativity of Christ," Robert Southwell.

25 "After Great Pain," Emily Dickinson, written in 1862.

26 *On Pilgrimage*, Dorothy Day. (Grand Rapids, MI: Wm. B. Eerdmans Publishing Co., 1997), p. 205.

27 *Life Secrets*, Henry Foster. (Brewster, MA: Paraclete Press, 1995), p. 119.

BIBLIOGRAPHY

❧

RECOMMENDED PRAYER BOOKS

For companions to, or independently of,
Daily Prayers for Times of Grief:

George Appleton, general editor, *The Oxford Book of Prayer* (Oxford/New York: Oxford University Press, 1985). Over 1,000 years of prayers, including those about death—several from faiths other than Christianity.

Companions for the Journey series (Winona, MN: St. Mary's Press, Christian Brothers Publications, 1995). Titles include *Praying with Hildegard* and *Praying with John of the Cross*.

John Carden, compiler, *A Procession of Prayers: Meditations and Prayers from Around the World* (Harrisburg, PA: Morehouse Publishing, 1998). The life of Jesus in prayers collected by an Anglican priest who has served in several cultures.

Church of the Province of New Zealand, *A New Zealand Prayer Book: He Karakia Mihinare O Aotearoa* (1997). Firmly within the Anglican tradition, yet distinguished by directness of language and modern, sound psychology.

ACKNOWLEDGMENTS

The making of any book represents the love of many people. This one is no exception. The love I felt as a small child, cuddled in the lap of my language-loving maternal grandmother, Effie Alice Hert Jackson, is here. The love of my own child, Edward Lane Hamilton, whose understanding of the world and of his mother staggers her, is here as well.

To the following contributors of ideas and criticism, I owe a special thanks: The Rev. Jamie Callaway, Dr. Peter Hawkins, Dr. Elizabeth Koenig, Sister Mary Michael, SSM, Alice Mindrum, The Rev. Fred Rogers, Robert Owens Scott, The Rev. Janna Tull Steed, and Sarah Watson Lovejoy and her family.

I am also especially appreciative of Phyllis Tickle, who believed enough in me to introduce me to her friends and colleagues at Paraclete Press, now mine as well: Dr. Lillian Miao and Sr. Mercy Minor.

I deeply appreciate the friends whose love did not end with Scott's death. You kept me from ending, and you and the friends with whom God has blessed me since make me glad indeed.

I am indebted to many, seen and unseen, living and dead, who have prayed this project to fruition. To God, I owe the most of all. May the words of this book and the meditations of our hearts be pleasing to our Creator, Redeemer, and Sustainer.

ABOUT PARACLETE PRESS

WHO WE ARE

Paraclete Press is a publisher of books, recordings, and DVDs on Christian spirituality. Our publishing represents a full expression of Christian belief and practice—from Catholic to Evangelical, from Protestant to Orthodox.

We are the publishing arm of the Community of Jesus, an ecumenical monastic community in the Benedictine tradition. As such, we are uniquely positioned in the marketplace without connection to a large corporation and with informal relationships to many branches and denominations of faith.

WHAT WE ARE DOING

BOOKS

Paraclete publishes books that show the richness and depth of what it means to be Christian. Although Benedictine spirituality is at the heart of all that we do, we publish books that reflect the Christian experience across many cultures, time periods, and houses of worship. We publish books that nourish the vibrant life of the church and its people—books about spiritual practice, formation, history, ideas, and customs.

We have several different series, including the best-selling Paraclete Essentials and Paraclete Giants series of classic texts in contemporary English; A Voice from the Monastery—men and women monastics writing about living a spiritual life today; award-winning poetry; best-selling gift books for children on the occasions of baptism and first communion; and the Active Prayer Series that brings creativity and liveliness to any life of prayer.

RECORDINGS

From Gregorian chant to contemporary American choral works, our music recordings celebrate sacred choral music through the centuries. Paraclete distributes the recordings of the internationally acclaimed choir Gloriæ Dei Cantores, praised for their "rapt and fathomless spiritual intensity" by *American Record Guide*, and the Gloriæ Dei Cantores Schola, which specializes in the study and performance of Gregorian chant. Paraclete is also the exclusive North American distributor of the recordings of the Monastic Choir of St. Peter's Abbey in Solesmes, France, long considered to be a leading authority on Gregorian chant.

VIDEOS

Our videos offer spiritual help, healing, and biblical guidance for life issues: grief and loss, marriage, forgiveness, anger management, facing death, and spiritual formation.

Learn more about us at our website:
www.paracletepress.com,
or call us toll-free at 1-800-451-5006.

SCAN
TO
READ
MORE

The Little Book of Hours

ISBN: 978-1-55725-533-4
$16.95, Trade paper

Experience the depth and beauty of an ancient prayer practice as it is celebrated in a modern monastic community

At the Church of the Transfiguration on Cape Cod, the Liturgy of the Hours is observed each day by the Community of Jesus, an ecumenical Christian community in the Benedictine monastic tradition. The Liturgy of the Hours is the heartbeat of everyday life, the pulse that sustains and nurtures the community. In this little book, all the richness of these ancient prayers is presented in a modified version for Christians everywhere. *The Little Book of Hours* provides four weeks of services, with three services for every day, and many additional collects and services. Learn how you can "pray the hours" in the midst of your busy life today.

Grieving: A Beginner's Guide

ISBN: 978-1-55725-493-1
$14.95, Trade paper

There is no sure route through grieving. Jerusha McCormack provides instead a series of signposts by which we may find our own path to a new life. "We are all amateurs at grief," she writes, "it comes to us all; we must all go through it. To treat grief as a problem to be fixed, or (worse still) to medicalize it, is to rob us of the extraordinary privilege of encountering this experience on our terms: for each of us has our own way of grieving, and each of us has something special to learn from the process."